How to be a
SCHOLAR

Smoothing the Transition from
High School to College...

and Beyond

THIRD EDITION

PAUL A. VERRELL ● NORAH R. MCCABE

Kendall Hunt
publishing company

CONTENTS

PREFACE TO THE THIRD EDITION

For a growing number of people, moving from high school to college and then college to career are two of life's biggest transitions. For many, they are also two of life's biggest challenges. This book is intended to help make both of these transitions, but especially the first, smoother than they might be otherwise. Based on our own experiences and our reading of relevant literature, we offer suggestions that are embedded in the context of the many and varied resources available at WSU that are there to help people like you to be as successful academically as you are able. Not all of our opinions may be shared by WSU's administration, and we thank our students, colleagues, reviewers, and publisher for encouragement and useful feedback.

We used the first edition of this book in a class consisting largely of first-year students in the fall of 2016. About one out of every two students told us that they found the book useful, although many also told us that they already knew a lot of what we wrote about. Interestingly, when asked at the end of the class what they could have done to have earned higher grades, most students' mentioned just the kinds of skills and habits that the book discussed, ones they said they already knew about. Here are some representative quotes from 2016 (we received almost identical comments from students who used the second edition of this book in 2017):

- "Study more."
- "Go to lecture."
- "Studied longer."
- "Be more attentive."
- "Taken better notes."
- "Went to office hours."
- "Created a study group."
- "Could have gotten tutoring."
- "Paid more attention in class."
- "Less time on my phone in class."
- "Could have started studying for tests earlier."

We don't intend to be mean, but it does seem that knowing something doesn't necessarily translate into positive action. We see this as a version of the so-called "double curse" recognized by psychologists David Dunning and Justin Kruger—not knowing what you don't really know, and so over-estimating how well you know what you don't really know (and besides, even if you really do know, surely it never hurts to be reminded).

We can understand why you might think that this book is unnecessary and a way for us authors to make money. However, we negotiated with our publisher to get the price of this book as low as possible—less than a week's worth of Starbucks lattes—and neither of us is earning a penny from its sales. That's not a whole lot of money, and we think it is a good deal even if only a modest outcome comes from such a modest outlay. And so we heartily invite you to explore further.

©Cartoonresource/Shutterstock.com

INTRODUCTION: ABOUT THIS BOOK

"Learning is not attained by chance, it must be sought for with ardor and diligence."

Abigail Adams, wife of President John Adams

"Chance favors the prepared mind."

Louis Pasteur, French scientist

"There are no secrets to success. It is the result of preparation, hard work, and learning from failure."

Colin Powell, US politician and military general

"Nothing worth having comes easy."

President Theodore Roosevelt

"Nothing will work unless you do."

Maya Angelou, novelist

"Nobody ever drowned in his own sweat."

Ann Landers, journalist and advice columnist

WHY WE WROTE IT

We live in a changing world in which competition within and among nations is intense, and a skilled workforce is needed more than ever before. Calls to increase the number of US citizens with at least some further education after high school are coming from many directions. Politicians tell us that additional education is crucial if our nation is to maintain a competitive edge in the global economy. Philanthropic organizations say the same thing. For example, the Lumina Foundation has the goal of increasing the proportion of the US workers with at least an associate degree to 60% by 2025. The Bill and Melinda Gates Foundation is calling for 22 million new college graduates by 2018. Additional education beyond high school is touted as the (well, *a*) key to gaining a middle-class life style. While a growing number of careers require training beyond high school, it should be remembered that not all require going to a four-year university such as WSU. One of us was once asked by a high school student whether WSU has a good engineering program (it does). When asked what kind of engineering he was interested in, the student replied that he wanted to work on repairing auto engines. There will always be a demand for engine mechanics, and for this person, a WSU degree in engineering might not be necessary, and perhaps a better path would be to take relevant classes at a community or technical college.

We think it is interesting and important to ask why students go to college. You might think this is a silly question—"For the jobs and the money!" That's not a bad reason—in 2013, the median difference in salary between employees with a high school diploma and those with a bachelor's degree was around $17,000. The economic advantage of a B.A. or B.S. remains even after accounting for the cost of attending college, perhaps in the form of loans to be repaid (with interest). That said, some bachelor's degrees result in higher payoffs than others, at least in the short term, such as computer science versus fine arts.

Money is important, but in addition to the quest to earn more, one might go to college to develop a more meaningful philosophy of life. A survey of Freshman conducted over the last 30 or so years has asked the extent to which dollars and ideas are very important or essential in terms of the reason for going to college. In 1983, nearly 69% of survey respondents rated dollars as being crucial—in 2013, that had risen to 82%. Ideas fared a bit less well. They were crucial for nearly 48% of respondents in 1983, but for only about 45% in 2013. We aren't so naïve as to think that college should be purely about philosophy, but we also think it should be about more than just job training, or what is sometimes called vocational training.

Regardless of why you choose to go to college, your goal surely is to be as successful as possible so that you can later attain the career goals you may already have or will develop shortly. However, all too often we see students fail to live up to their full potential. Low motivation and inadequate study skills can result in poor grades, which only lower motivation and performance further—it can become a vicious cycle. Students may leave college before graduating. Alternatively, they may graduate but with qualifications that aren't competitive in the work world they are about to enter. We wrote this book to encourage and help you to live up to your full potential, and so be successful in college and beyond.

Between the two of us, we have more than 50 years of experience teaching and advising undergraduate and graduate students, just over 50 of those years at WSU. We've worked with undergraduates ranging from first-years to seniors, and with both science and nonscience majors (we're both biologists). We've taught classes consisting of as many as 730 students to classes as small as a dozen. And so, based on our experiences, we asked ourselves: "What does a student need to know in order to be successful in college and beyond?" As we started to make a list, we realized two things. First, our list would be a very long one. Second, our theme needed to be more specific. And so, we asked a new question: "How can a student make the transition from high school to college as successful as possible, especially in terms of academics?" What advice can we share?

High school is behind you and your first semester in college is about to begin. What will it take for you to be a successful student?

©Ermolaev Alexander/Shutterstock.com

HOW WE WROTE IT

We did not set out to write a how-to guide on all of the things that a college student needs to know in order to thrive—first this, second that, third something else, etc. If you want a list of how-to guides, and it will be a long one, check out Google and Amazon.com. And so, we say very little about managing finances and not too much about social relationships. Because our primary but not exclusive focus is on the transition from high school to college, we don't say very much about such topics as specific requirements for graduation and job planning. This isn't because we believe planning for graduation and beyond are unimportant, but we think other issues have priority early in a student's career.

There are lots of books out there that are all about telling you how to "game-the-system" academically (although that isn't how they refer to themselves). Our hope is that, rather than simply providing checklists on what to do to earn good grades, we encourage you to think about your present motivations, attitudes, and abilities, and how you might improve them in ways that will make you an effective learner in college and beyond. And we want you to continue thinking along these lines from the first weeks in your first year to your final weeks as a senior (and so, we think that sophomores, juniors, and seniors will benefit from reading this book). This kind of self-reflection, sometimes called metacognition, might be uncomfortable and even painful at times, but it can fundamentally change the way you think and how you learn. In short, we hope to convince you that college is about more than getting A grades.

This is a book *about* academics, not a book written *for* academics, and so we have not included citations to relevant literature, such as books and articles in journals (you, on the other hand, will *always* be expected to include such citations in what you write in college). In addition, we've written our text in a style that is rather conversational (something that you won't do in a lot of your own writing in college). Our hope is that this makes our text more readable. We have included numerical data where we think they are appropriate, largely to provide evidence to support the suggestions we make. And while we had WSU students specifically in mind as we wrote this book, we think that our discussions and recommendations are of use across all of the diverse institutions that comprise higher education in the United States. These include four-year universities such as WSU (teaching and research) and liberal arts colleges (mainly teaching), as well as two-year community colleges and vocational or technical colleges (teaching only).

However, because you are a WSU student, go to your favorite electronic device immediately and bookmark this page: www.conduct.wsu.edu/resources. This website provides URLs and other contact information for a wide variety of WSU- and local community-based programs and organizations that every one of you should be aware of. No matter what kind of help or advice you may seek (and we all need help at times—health, academic, legal, and other), this website is an extremely valuable resource. Next, bookmark the site of the Academic Success and Career Center (ASCC): www.ascc.wsu.edu. The ASCC can help academically in almost every way—advising, counseling, mentoring, tutoring, and so much more. Finally, bookmark WSU's Cougar Success site, which is full of good advice on various academic issues, from taking notes to taking exams: www.cougarsuccess .wsu.edu.

We believe college should be an enjoyable and satisfying challenge. As you'll see, it won't be easy because it isn't meant to be easy—you should expect to be challenged and, with your dedicated effort and use of all the resources available to you, you will meet and overcome those challenges.

HOW TO USE IT

While written primarily for students who have entered WSU straight from high school and who are in their first year, we believe that *all* undergraduates will benefit from considering the ideas we present and the suggestions we make. Most chapters end with a worksheet designed to encourage you to reflect honestly on your own learning (this is metacognition, as we mentioned earlier). We want to encourage you to detach these worksheets and collate them in a ring binder so that, by the end of the semester, you will have created a "learning portfolio." This should serve as a useful reference as you complete your degree, and perhaps you could share it with others. Some instructors may require you to complete and submit these worksheets as part of class requirements, perhaps for graded credit.

OK, let's get started! Let's explore some ways by which you might smooth the transition from high school to college . . . and beyond.

IN 2018, MORE THAN 90,000 FIRST-YEAR U.S. COLLEGE STUDENTS WERE SURVEYED ABOUT WHAT KINDS OF HELP WOULD RESULT IN THEM FEELING A GREATER SENSE OF CONNECTION AND BELONGING, BOTH ACADEMICALLY AND SOCIALLY. HERE'S SOME OF WHAT THEY SAID

- *Finding new friends: 71% of respondents*
- *Taking exams: 69%*
- *Developing study habits: 67%*
- *Exploring clubs and social organizations: 67%*
- *Finding a scholarship: 65%*
- *Meeting experienced students to act as mentors: 55%*
- *Exploring student government: 53%*
- *Matching interests to careers: 52%*
- *Sharpening math and writing skills: 50%*
- *Finding tutoring: 47%*
- *Sharpening reading skills: 36%*
- *Counseling for various personal issues: 7-18%*

ABOUT THE AUTHORS

Paul Verrell is an Associate Professor (biological sciences) and Norah McCabe is a Clinical Associate Professor (molecular biosciences) at Washington State University (WSU). Both earned Ph.D. degrees, in animal behavior and neurochemistry, respectively, in England before moving to the United States in 1986. They worked as researchers at the University of Chicago until 1993, when they moved to WSU. With more than 50 years of combined experience in working with US undergraduates and graduates as award-winning instructors, research mentors, and academic advisors (and with two post-college sons), they wrote this book to provide evidence-based recommendations for maximizing academic success in those crucial early semesters in college. Full of relevant information on the various support services offered by the university, this book serves as a reference for the integration and use of all these resources. By completing worksheets provided at the end of each chapter, students will be fully engaged, and they will finish the book with a portfolio that will be useful as they transition from high school students to college scholars, and beyond.

CHAPTER 1
ARE *YOU* UP TO THE CHALLENGE?

You went through the process of applying to colleges where you thought there'd be a good fit between you and them. For some people, the fit is an academic one; for others, the fit might be financial, cultural, or geographic. You thought really hard about what you want from your college experience. A good fit and future promise for success are among the things that your college admissions officers looked for in the application materials you sent. You thought this institution would be a good fit. And what you wrote worked, because WSU agreed and now you're here.

©Efired/Shutterstock.com

WHO AM I?

18 or 19 years of age
Just a bit more likely to be female
Very likely to be a Washington resident
A high school GPA of around 3.4
Composite SAT score of around 1060

I'm a first-year WSU student

Yes, you're here. Your dorm room is a bit small for all the stuff you brought but your roommate(s) seems nice (unmarried students under the age of 20 years must live on campus). The food isn't bad—lots of choices and some of it is "all-you-can-eat." Better be careful of those extra pounds though (there are healthy options available). You must remember to pick up your books and other supplies at The Bookie. Classes start next week and you're going to be ready.

Higher education is a business and colleges compete for good students. Well, let's be even more honest and more accurate—colleges compete for your dollars, and we'd rather you spend your money here than elsewhere. All colleges produce glossy materials designed to be persuasive—"Look at our great dorms! Look at our great Rec Center! Look at all of our student clubs!" Perhaps unintentionally, the academic aspect of college can sometimes get a bit drowned out.

The primary reason you are here is the academic one. You are here to learn—even learn how to learn, something that will go on for a lifetime. Your goal is to consider new ideas, challenge old ones, and prepare yourself for what comes next. And all of that is going to be at times enjoyable, frustrating, stressful, and challenging (but ultimately it will be worth it, and you should be excited about that).

Don't just take our word for it. A few years ago, we conducted a survey of nearly 700 WSU students, 70% of them first-years and sophomores, in two 100-level biology classes, one for biology majors and one not (there were more of the latter). We asked these students to tell us how challenging they were finding their academic work at WSU. Let's stress here that we were asking students to self-reflect and give us their opinions. Here's a summary of their responses:

- More challenging than I expected: 51% of students.
- About what I expected: 41%.
- Less challenging than I expected: 8%.

Remember that many of these students were new to college. About one out of every two respondents told us that they found their academic work to be more challenging than they expected. Your peers are talking to you here, and they're telling you to expect to be challenged. The data are telling us and you that college isn't the same as high school.

"I'll pause for your moans and groans."

©Cartoonresource/Shutterstock.com

To explore these self-reflections further, we asked the students how well they felt their high schools had prepared them for college. We'd guess that the better the preparation in high school is, the better able the students should be to rise to the academic challenge of college work. Here's what they told us:

- I feel well prepared: 70% of respondents.
- I feel poorly prepared: 28%.
- I don't know: 2%.

We then dug a little deeper because that last question was rather broad. We asked students to tell us how well prepared they felt in terms of particular study skills and what are known as "habits of mind." Think of the latter as attitudes that are important for success in college and beyond. There are a lot of numbers coming next, but we encourage you to examine them. Following are the students' evaluations of their degrees of preparedness (poor, adequate, or well):

	Poor	Adequate	Well
Complete all work	6	17	77
Be ethical	9	15	76
Take pride in good work	7	18	75
Be prepared for class	9	18	73
Attend class	8	20	72
Communicate well	15	25	60
Be responsible	16	25	59
Like to be challenged	15	28	57
Persevere	15	30	55
Be curious	15	31	54
Attend to detail	19	33	48
Go beyond the minimum	22	32	46
Use additional resources	26	33	41
Manage time	35	29	36
Study to deeply learn	34	35	31

What we see from these numbers is that only about a half or fewer of our respondents said they were well prepared in such crucial skills or habits as attending to detail, managing time, and studying to deeply learn. These aren't just crucial for success throughout your time in college—they're crucial for career success, too.

Surveys often ask the same question more than once, but in different ways, to check for consistency of responses. And so, we asked our students what skills or habits they wish they had practiced more of in high school. We didn't give them prompts in terms of specific answers because we didn't want our opinions to bias their responses. Here's what they said:

- Time management: 48% of respondents.
- Exam preparation: 39%.
- Thinking independently: 27%.
- Writing: 16%.
- Studying to understand: 12%.
- Subject knowledge: 11%.
- Reading: 10%.

We'll show you just one more set of numbers. We asked our students what skills or habits they wanted to develop further in the current semester. With no prompts given, they responded:

- Time management: 40% of respondents.
- Exam preparation: 39%.
- Think independently: 15%.
- Writing: 13%.

- Subject knowledge: 9%.
- Reading: 8%.
- Study to understand or remember: 8%.

These are a lot of numbers, and fortunately you don't need to remember them. But do appreciate what your peers are telling you. They are telling you that they were challenged by college, but thought, overall, that they were prepared. When pushed a bit, your peers recognized certain areas where they were less prepared. Most of those areas don't surprise us as instructors and academic advisors, but it is important to remember that your peers realized these potential shortcomings for themselves. Time management was the Number One challenge they recognized—a skill that close to half of the students felt they didn't have and also one that they wanted to develop further. We'll explore this further in Chapter Three.

Effective time management is a skill many students wish they had developed further before starting college.

©Aquir/Shutterstock.com

In summary, your peers (not parents and not instructors) are telling you that college isn't 13th grade and that you will be challenged academically more than you might expect. The data given above provided the trigger we needed to write this book. What advice can we offer you in terms of meeting challenges by smoothing the pathway from high school to college and, ultimately, to career?

IN 2016, ANNE CURZAN OF THE UNIVERSITY OF MICHIGAN ASKED HER STUDENTS WHAT THEY DO TO LEARN EFFECTIVELY. HERE ARE SOME OF HER STUDENTS' RESPONSES

- *Come to class prepared.*
- *Ask for help if or when you need it.*
- *Remember that your instructors are human, too.*
- *Focus on learning, not just getting good grades.*
- *Be an active participant in the learning process.*
- *Ask good questions, and lots of them [our emphasis on "good"].*
- *Connect with your class-mates, listen to one another, and be respectful.*
- *Expect that sometimes things will be difficult and you'll make mistakes, but move forward.*
- *Go to office hours and connect with your professor, and not just when you have problems.*

WORKSHEET 1
READ: ARE *YOU* UP TO THE CHALLENGE?

"Learning is not attained by chance, it must be sought for with ardor and diligence."
Abigail Adams, wife of President John Adams

1. List four ways in which you expect university courses to be the *same* as high school courses, and give reasons.

    a.

    b.

    c.

    d.

2. List four ways in which you expect university courses to be *different* from high school courses, and give reasons.

    a.

    b.

    c.

    d.

3. Design a timetable that will be called Timetable One throughout the book. This will cover days starting on Monday morning and ending on Sunday night.

Include time you expect to spend in classes, the time you expect to spend studying, the time you expect to spend relaxing, and the time you expect to spend sleeping.

Please leave extra room for editing Timetable One as you will copy it and fill it out later when requested with your *actual* time spent.

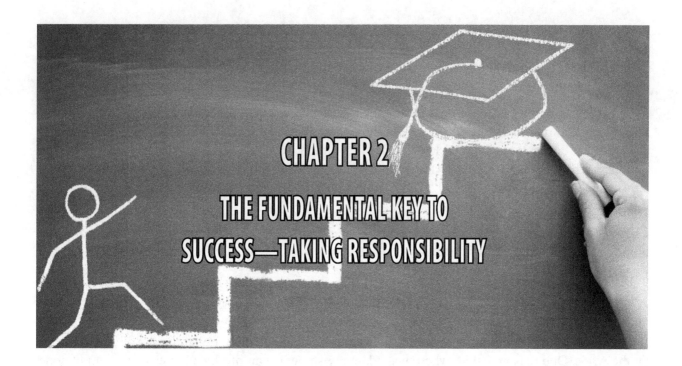

CHAPTER 2

THE FUNDAMENTAL KEY TO
SUCCESS—TAKING RESPONSIBILITY

If this is your first year at WSU and you came here straight from high school, then you are a member of the class of 2022. Congratulations! If you complete all you need to do by May 2022, then you will be the proud owner of a bachelor's degree in four years.

But there's a catch, sometimes referred to as the "aspiration-achievement gap." Recent data show that about one in five students reading these words at the start of their first semester will leave WSU at the end of their first year, a number close to the national average. And historical data suggest that only about three or four in 10 of you will actually graduate in 2022, four years after you start your studies (almost all of our degree programs should, in principle, last no longer than four years). For full-time, first-time college students at public universities, the national average for graduation rates in six years—that's how they calculate the number at the national level—was about 59% for the Class of 2013. For WSU's class of 2011, that number was 62%. We think you'll agree that these are disappointing numbers.

Why, at the national level, do four out of every ten first-time, full-time students (people like most of you) fail to earn a bachelor's degree within six years? We can think of two kinds of reasons, both of which could be making a contribution.

INTELLECTUAL PREPARATION AND ACADEMIC ABILITY

All of you came to WSU with a high school GPA (an average of 3.39 out of 4.0), and most of you came with SAT rather than ACT scores. The SAT is not intended to measure student achievement as much as serve as a predictor of success in college—data show that the old SAT (there's now a new version) is a better predictor for some student populations and for some institutions, but overall neither it nor high school GPA are so great at predicting college GPA (although high school GPA is better). Here's one final statistic—based on new SAT scores for 2017, only 46% of high school graduates were considered to be ready for college in English and math.

It isn't too surprising that some instructors feel that students aren't adequately prepared and/or not able to succeed intellectually in college. At the national level, this has encouraged the development of somewhat contentious national High School Common Core educational standards, developed so far in English Language Arts and Mathematics. Here at WSU, we have developed a number of math classes that are at the precollege level and are designed to help students catch up.

There seems to be a mismatch between what students appear to be achieving before college, at least GPA-wise (and high school GPAs have been rising steadily over the last few years), and what some fail to achieve after they matriculate into a place like WSU. The big questions are: why, and what can we do about it?

ATTITUDE AND MOTIVATION

We do not think that poor college performance can be blamed solely on students not being able to do the work. One reason is that, when pushed, many students can produce better work than they do otherwise. We almost used the word "encouraged" rather than pushed, but that wouldn't be entirely accurate. Sometimes a big push is needed (not literally, of course).

Why is encouragement and pushing needed? There's a pretty strong consensus among college instructors that our rush to build self-esteem in K-12 education has led to the belief that everyone can win and that trying hard isn't always necessary. Everyone in K-12 wins a medal or a certificate—best grades, most popular, most altruistic, etc. But college doesn't work that way. You *do* have to put effort in, and even with your best effort there's no guarantee of success. As instructors we don't *give* you grades—as students you *earn* them. We believe that, thanks to this notion that "everyone's a winner," too many students coming straight from high school haven't had the chance to develop the right attitude and motivation to do well. Too many students come to college feeling entitled to good grades regardless of how hard they do or don't study.

In addition, students risk developing some bad habits during their final year of high school. Students fail to attend class regularly. They become careless about their work, putting off assignments until the last minute. You might recognize apathy, truancy, and procrastination as the symptoms of "senioritis." In 12th grade, you have at least some idea of where you are going next, and so you might just coast.

Here are some numbers that we think are disappointing, to say the least. They come from a national survey of first-year college students who were asked what they did in 12th grade. A few responses include:

- 28% of respondents skipped their classes.
- 52% skipped doing homework.
- 58% studied five hours or less per week outside of class (remember this because we'll talk about it later).

These numbers cast light on the results of a 2015 Gallup survey of high school students. Only 34% of 12th graders said they were engaged with their studies. Furthermore, only 23% of juniors said they were excited about learning and had a positive vision for their future.

The danger is that high school senioritis can mutate, like some terrible virus, into college "fresh-manitis." With a relaxed attitude toward academic work and a huge array of social opportunities to choose from, some students see college as a place to have fun, "fireworks fun," where every day is like a 4th of July party.

College isn't meant to be "fireworks fun." It should be a satisfying and enjoyable challenge.

National data for 2014 reveal the biggest danger that can develop from college freshmanitis. Take a look at this graph, in which six-year graduation rate is plotted against first-year GPA. Remember that almost all bachelor's degree programs are designed to be completed within four years, not six:

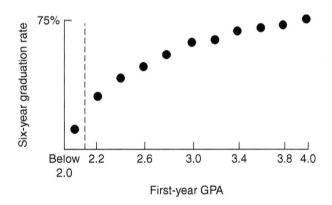

With a first-year GPA below 2.0 (which means that a WSU student is academically deficient), just 12% of students graduated in six years. That number rose to the highest six-year graduation rate of 74% for students whose first-year GPA was a perfect 4.0.

What these data surely do is to destroy a myth that too many college students believe. We've heard students say "It's OK if I goof around in my first year. It's how well I do later that really counts." Take a look at those graduation rates again, and you can see the importance of your first-year GPA. You can't afford to develop college freshmanitis, and the key to avoiding it is to take responsibility from Day One onward.

HOW GOOD ARE FIRST-YEAR STUDENTS AT PREDICTING THEIR SHORT-TERM ACADEMIC SUCCESS?

In the fall of 2016, we helped WSU alumna Brandi Heath, then at Central Michigan University, to answer a very important question—how well do WSU first-year students' perceptions of their college readiness from high school predict their performance in college exams? Conducting this research was a requirement for Brandi's M.S. degree in Research Administration.

Brandi surveyed first-year first-semester students in a large non-majors science class to determine individual opinions of how well their high schools had prepared them academically for college. Although most students told Brandi they felt that they had been prepared quite well, the answer to her thesis question was "no." Statistically speaking, self-reported scores of degree of college readiness did not predict exam performance for WSU students—they weren't even close. For example, both the highest (96%) and lowest (39%) scoring students reported that they felt adequately prepared, with average or better self-assessments of their academic abilities.

Overall, Brandi concluded that most students over-estimated their preparedness for work at the college level. Thinking that you know something well when actually you don't is what we termed the "double curse" in our Preface. It is also known as the illusion of explanatory depth, and Brandi thinks it was at work in the students that she studied. What's most important is that over-estimating your competence can lead to performance problems which may then dent your confidence, and result in anxiety and even depression. For some students, such negative feelings may lead them to leave college.

MONEY MATTERS

We should say a few words about money. For some first-year students especially, careful budgeting is a bit unfamiliar, so start cautiously and proceed carefully. First, be sure you know what's going into your bank account—it may be some mixture of scholarships, grants, loans, savings, and money from Mom and Dad. Second, be very sure you know what's coming out (books, food, entertainment, etc). Remember that you're starting to build your credit history, and that your choices now impact you down the line in terms of interest rates when borrowing to buy, say, a car or an apartment (talk to your bank manager: you're looking to find a balance between owing money, but not too much, and paying your debts). Third, spend thoughtfully, especially if spending will increase your debt. A trip to Fort Lauderdale for Spring Break might sound very tempting, but is it a wise use of your funds? Finally, shop around before choosing a bank. For example, some charge you to take your money out of an ATM and others don't, or they charge less.

THE RESPONSIBLE STUDENT

If you want your college experience to be a "fireworks fun" party that lasts for four years or, more likely, longer, then that's certainly possible as long as you maintain a GPA of 2.0 (the minimum needed for graduation). But will graduating with a GPA of 2.0 win you that place in law school? Or your dream job with a software development company (or *any* job that requires a bachelor's degree)? What you need to do, in a way that may be unfamiliar and even uncomfortable, is to take responsibility for yourself, going well beyond the minimum required and always looking to the future. This is the fundamental key to success, not just in college but in life.

The challenges recognized by the students in our survey were all academic, and they're the ones we'll focus on in this book. But of course, they aren't the only challenges faced by individuals who may be away from home and on their own for the first time. Now you have to negotiate challenges such as balancing your check book and making wise social choices. While these challenges are real and important, we must add to them the challenge of taking responsibility for your own learning. While we don't just throw you to the wolves as a college student, we do expect you to shoulder some essential responsibilities. Think of it like this. There's a whole team of people working with you to help you become as successful as you are able. But every team needs a captain, a leader who takes ultimate responsibility for all that is achieved, the good and the not-so-good. We want each one of you to be a responsible captain of your team.

©Hxdbzxy/Shutterstock.com

A responsible student both attends class and participates in it. Got a question? Put your hand up—you're certainly not alone, and students who ask questions are recognized and appreciated by their instructors.

Take a look at the E-mail below that was sent to one of us in the fall of 2016. All we've done is to blank-out the identifiers. We show it to you not to be horrid and nasty, but to stress the importance of taking responsibility. Here it is:

"Dear Professor WWW,

Hello my name is XXX and I am in your YYY class. This past weekend I went home and forgot to take into account that we have a test on Monday. I am still at home and am not going to be able to make it to Pullman by 9 a.m. tomorrow. Is there a chance that I could reschedule the test for later in the week? If so, I would greatly appreciate it. I am sorry for this inconvenience.

Sincerely,

ZZZ"

Imagine that, instead of writing to his professor, this student had written these words to his employer. What do you think his boss might have replied? "That's OK, you just stay home for as long as you like," perhaps?

Here's just one more example of a student behaving carelessly, provided, as was the first, to underscore the importance of being responsible. In the spring of 2017 we found a missing entry in our class grade-book. We wrote to the student to ask if she would send us the exam score we had apparently lost. But we hadn't lost it. Here's what she wrote:

> "Hi,

I'm sorry, I actually missed the first exam. I overslept that day and didn't make it in.

> Thanks, XXX"

Given the value of that first exam (and her score of zero), this student could earn no higher than a C+ even if she aced all other class assignments.

SO LET'S GET STARTED

As you'll see time and time again in this book, and as revealed earlier in those data from your peers, college isn't just an extension of high school. It may sound trivial, but in college there's no one around to make sure that you're doing what you need to do when it needs to be done. It is all up to you to take responsibility for your actions and inactions. Our goal here is to show you why being a responsible student matters, and to give you some pointers as to how you can boost your academic success to levels that you might not reach otherwise. And the good news is that it really isn't as difficult as you might think. Well, let's reword that. The ideas aren't hard to grasp, but putting them into action will take some effort, even a bit of sweat.

A QUICK GUIDE TO QUESTIONS A RESPONSIBLE STUDENT WOULD *NEVER* ASK

- *Where's your office?*
- *When's the next test?*
- *Will this be on the test?*
- *When is the paper due?*
- *Why did you give me a D?*
- *Office hours? What are they?*
- *Office hours? When are they?*
- *What is your E-mail address?*
- *What is my TA's E-mail address?*
- *What kind of extra credit is available?*
- *You mean there's a syllabus for this class?*
- *I missed class. Did you cover anything important?*
- *Can I give you my paper tomorrow instead of today?*
- *I went to most of your lectures, so how could I have failed?*
- *You mean even though I stopped going to class I was still enrolled?*
- *Can you write me a letter of recommendation by tomorrow morning?*

WORKSHEET 2
READ: THE FUNDAMENTAL KEY TO SUCCESS—TAKING RESPONSIBILITY

The big take-home message is that your instructors are responsible for teaching the material and you are responsible for learning it. This is a very dynamic, but rather unequal, partnership. Your instructor *knows and teaches* the content (he or she has probably been teaching the course for at least a few years), and it is up to you to *understand and learn* the content. Instructors are also humans—some days they're tired, lack motivation, and feel overworked, underpaid, and underappreciated. Perhaps your instructor just looked at a social media site wherein he or she was criticized for the clothes he or she wore or was referred to as a moron (yes, such comments are made: take a look at RateMyProfessors). He or she is really upset and so his or her teaching isn't quite up to scratch. Life happens, even to instructors.

Here are two scenarios, and for each, with honesty, write a paragraph on what you might be *tempted* to do and another paragraph on what you *should do and why*.

1. Scenario One. Your instructor was obviously tired or fed-up or perhaps ill today, and he or she contradicted himself or herself and was totally disorganized. You were really confused when you left the lecture, as were other students.

   a. What would you be tempted to do?

   b. What *should* you do and why?

2. Scenario Two. Your instructor has strongly advised that you study after each lecture—for at least one hour and sometimes for as much as three hours for every 50-minute lecture, or until you "get it."

a. What would you be tempted to do?

b. What *should* you do and why?

Please make and attach a copy of Timetable One from Worksheet One and modify or edit it to reflect your actual timetable during the last week (be honest).

Remember that, in our survey, about one out of every two respondents said that time management was an important challenge to their college success. We agree. But the important thing is that students themselves, your peers, realized this. It is *their* words you read, not *ours*. So how can you manage your time as effectively as possible?

Meet Mary. Mary is in her senior year of high school. She plays basketball and the cello, and she's also a cheerleader for the football team. Plus she's studying for the SAT when not working as a part-time baby sitter on weekends. Mary is busy, but the responsibility for effectively managing her time is shared with Mom, Dad, her older sister, and her coach. They make sure that Mary gets to where she needs to be when she needs to be there. Her teachers also help, as does her school counselor. Late work is accepted, deadlines are somewhat flexible, and extra credit is given for submitting work on time.

But when Mary goes to college, managing her time effectively will no longer be a shared responsibility. It will be Mary's responsibility, and her's alone. Mary will have to make sure that all the things she *needs* to do and all the things she *wants* to do (not necessarily the same things) fit into the time available—there are few to no flexible deadlines in college. Do remember that the results of our survey revealed that about one out of every two students saw managing time effectively as the biggest challenge they face.

KNOW WHAT YOU NEED TO DO AND WHEN

Effective time management needs to be achieved at three levels: by day, by week, and by semester. For each day in the week you must know where you need to be and when. Here's a hypothetical class schedule (we've left out the labs for the two science classes):

- Biology 102: M, W, F, 9.10–10.00 AM.
- English 101: M, W, F, 1.10–2.00 PM.

- Chemistry 101: M, W, F, 2.10–3.00 PM.
- Anthropology 101: Tu, Th, 2.50–4.05 PM.

At registration time, check whether the classes you want have multiple sections. For example, Biology 102 in the fall semester of 2017 had two lecture sections, identical in content, the second from 10.10 to 11 AM. If you aren't much of a "morning person," then a start later than 9.10 may have been the better choice.

Now you can start to schedule study groups, trips to the gym, and times to hang out with friends. On a day-to-day basis, you can remind yourself what you need to accomplish with handy to-do lists. At the week-to-semester level, you'll need some kind of planner to ensure that you know due-dates for assignments and when exams will be held.

©Syda Productions/Shutterstock.com

> *In college, time is of the essence. You have to know what you need to do in order to fit in what you want to do. If you don't, the consequence may be academic deficiency.*

Every student's best friends in college are the syllabi provided for each class. Whether given to you on paper or made available online, a syllabus provides crucial information that you need to know. Your instructor took time to write the syllabus, and you must take time to read it and *understand* it. In the context of time management, perhaps the most important things you should consider are:

- Just when particular topics will be covered in lectures, so that you can review relevant material beforehand.
- The dates when particular assignments are due, such as papers.
- The dates of important quizzes and exams.

We hear it all the time. "But I thought the paper was due *next* Friday, not *this* Friday!" "Is the exam short essay or multiple choice?" We shouldn't hear these things at all, because the relevant information is in the syllabus. The problem is that too few students read it carefully. Imagine you are working in an accounting firm, and you ask your boss a question that he or she spent a lot of time and effort answering earlier. You might not have your job for much longer.

Simply put, you have to know what you need to do and when you need to do it. Then you can make choices, prioritizing those things that you decide need your most urgent attention. Whether you put this important information into a smartphone or write it on a big wall calendar doesn't matter. You need to make sure that the information is recorded in a place where you will look at it—be *forced* to look at it, if necessary. Only when you know what needs to be done and when for all of your classes can you schedule the things you want to do. Only when you know what needs to be done can you start prioritizing tasks. Remember, just because an assignment is due far off into the future doesn't mean you should postpone thinking about it, especially if that assignment is an important one (say, a big chunk of your final grade). Your priorities may change over time, of course. For example, hanging out with friends is something you should put off if a big exam is looming ahead.

As instructors we take deadlines seriously, and not because we are mean and horrible. True, some of us may be more flexible than others, but no deadlines or deadlines that are too flexible can result in chaos, which is bad for everyone. Each fall one of us teaches a class that may have an enrollment of more than 700 students. Can you imagine what having no or loose deadlines for papers and exams would be like in a class of that size?

We take deadlines seriously for another reason. Flexibility almost certainly won't always exist in your real world of jobs. If your boss wants the financial report on his or her desk today, he or she means today and not tomorrow. By enforcing deadlines now we are getting you in the right mind-set for avoiding problems later.

We aren't mean and horrible, and we realize that, even with good time management skills, your best plans can get waylaid. Perhaps you are an athlete, and there's a time conflict between a midterm history exam and a baseball game in Corvallis. You can't help it if the stomach flu strikes the night before your chemistry final. There are legitimate reasons why you might sometimes miss deadlines, and your instructors may work with you to provide opportunities for earning points that might otherwise be lost. But we stress that these are special cases, and that not knowing what needs to be done and when is not a valid excuse.

EFFECTIVE STUDYING TAKES TIME

College students tend to underestimate the amount of time they need to study. It isn't unusual for us to hear a student say how hard he or she studied for an exam. When we ask "How long?" that student might reply, with pride, "Three or four hours."

WSU is the only college in Washington to maintain an academic calendar of two semesters of instruction per academic year (two semesters of 16 weeks each—this omits summer school). Most students at WSU average 15 credits of coursework per semester (15 credits in each of eight semesters—four years—sums to a total of 120 credits, the minimum required for graduation. But don't overload yourself by piling on credits—in academics, the winner is the person who finishes *best*, not *first*.). You'll often see this referred to as 15 credit-hours, which might lead you to think that 15 credits requires only 15 hours of study per week. But you'd be very wrong. A three-credit course at WSU typically has no lab and consists of three 50-minute (or two 75-minute) lectures per week. A science class for four credits typically has three 50-minute lectures and one three-hour lab. All classes may include formal discussion groups. And so, for a student taking two science and two UCORE classes, in-class time could be around 18 hours, maybe more.

But that number doesn't include the time you need to spend studying outside of class. You'll be writing papers and lab reports. Preparing for exams. Reading your textbook and other sources of information. There's a rule-of-thumb that says you should study around three hours *out* of class for every hour you are *in* class. If you do the math you'll see the total time you should invest in 15 credits worth of classes far exceeds 15 hours per week—it could be up to 60 hours, which is more than a full-time job (with no overtime pay). To put it all in a broader perspective, a recent national study found that the average US college student invested about 14 hours of study time outside of class.

©Cartoonresource/Shutterstock.com

Here are some data that stress more intensely the importance of taking enough time to study. Have a look at this graph:

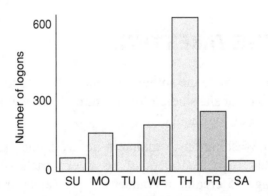

You are looking at the number of visits over one week to a website that included PowerPoints, lecture outlines, and sample questions in a class of 711 students. The third exam in this class was held on a Friday (shown in dark gray). Note how few visits occurred Sunday through Wednesday. The highest number of visits over this seven-day period occurred on Thursday, *one day before the exam*. The second highest number occurred on *the day of the exam*, which started at 9 AM (not a whole lot of time to prepare if you also want to sleep, which you should do before an exam). The median letter grade for this exam was C-, meaning that 50% of the class earned that grade or lower. At the level of the whole class, we can only conclude one or maybe both of two things. First, the majority of students didn't or couldn't budget their time effectively. Second, at least some students didn't really care about the grade they would earn. We hope you are as disappointed as we are and that you listen to what research suggests. All-nighters and other kinds of quick learning don't foster long-term retention of information.

HOW GOOD ARE YOU AT PREDICTING YOUR EXAM PERFORMANCE?

We discussed earlier the research of Brandi Heath, who found that self-reported scores of degree of college readiness did not predict exam performance for first-year WSU students in a large non-majors science class. In fact they weren't even close. Brandi concluded with a lot of data and from many analyses that most students over-estimated their preparedness for work at the college level.

What do you think about your likely performance this semester? The Table below asks you to enter your scores for two exams early-ish in the semester and for your final exam for up to four classes (more than four would be an overload, we think). It also asks you to predict your final grade (A-F) after completing two exams, and to enter your actual final grade. When all the data are in, be reflective and ask yourself: did my exam scores change over time? Did my actual grades match the ones I predicted earlier in the semester? Am I satisfied with my performance, and if not, why? What could I have done differently?

Class name	First exam %	Second exam %	Predicted final grade after two exams	Final exam %	Actual final grade

---

JUGGLING MULTIPLE BALLS

We must also consider *quality* of study time, not just *quantity*. One aspect of quality that has been studied scientifically is multitasking, trying to attend to multiple tasks at the same time. You might be reading a textbook, listening to music, checking Twitter, and talking on the phone all at once, for example. You might believe that you're good at multitasking but you're almost certainly worse than you think. A recent study found that, even for students who entered college with high ACT scores (i.e., high achievers), academic performance was lowered when students surfed the Web in class for nonclass reasons. Another study found that students spend about 20% of class time on some form of electronic device. When asked why, the reasons given included boredom, entertainment, staying connected socially, and studying for other classes. And this is despite the fact that these same students told the researchers doing the study that they were quite aware that using such devices in these ways could hurt their grades. In the same way as you shouldn't text while driving, you shouldn't text during class. It is true that strategies exist that that can help you to become a better multi-tasker (albeit sequentially rather than simultaneously), but we suggest that you put them off until later.

What if you need to take a job while you are in college? At the national level, about 70% of undergraduates work while attending college (some work more than others, of course). Some students have to work because otherwise they simply couldn't afford tuition, fees, books, housing, food, etc. Whether you choose to work, perhaps to gain useful experience, or you need to work to pay the bills, here's our advice. First, keep the number of hours that you work as low as you can, especially in your first one or two semesters. It may be difficult, but you have to find a balance between working to pay the bills and working to do well in your classes. Second, try to find a job that is relevant to your interests and career goals.

FUNCTIONAL STUDY GROUPS

A good way to keep on track is by working with friends. There are data to show that the amount of time students study alone predicts their academic performance. But studying with friends also has value (we'd just say don't *only* study in groups). Meeting regularly to discuss class work encourages you to manage your time carefully, but be sure to spend that time wisely. We often see study groups in which everyone sits at a table, reading his or her books, and occasionally marking them with highlighter pens. This isn't what we call a "functional study group." In such a group people actively challenge one another. Perhaps you are asked to explain how Chopin's piano sonatas differ from those of Beethoven. If your answer isn't satisfactory, the members of a functional study group will tell you so and push you to provide a better answer. Similarly with papers—so-called peer review, in which you read one another's texts, can be very valuable. But feedback has to be honest and critical, not nastily so but constructively critical. Rather than simply say "This really is a bad piece of work," instead make suggestions for improvement. It can be hard to be critical of your friends' work—and hard to take criticism from them—but giving and taking criticism is a hallmark of a functional study group.

WSU makes it easy for students to create functional study groups. First-year students living in residence halls may find themselves sharing a course in common with a neighbor as part of the First-Year Focus program. In Academic Theme halls, students with similar academic interests live together. These different kinds of living-learning communities smooth the transition to college both academically and socially.

BE SMART

To finish up, we'll introduce you to a SMART way of thinking about setting goals that will help you manage your time more effectively. This way of thinking has been advocated by many educators, including ourselves, and it originated in the work of George T. Doran, Director of Corporate

Planning for Washington Water Power Company (now Avista Corporation). Here's the basic idea. For every task you are set, ask if you're being SMART:

- S = specific: just what is it that I'm trying to achieve?
- M = measurable: how will I know when I've achieved my goal?
- A = achievable: can I actually get the job done?
- R = relevant: how will attaining this goal meet my needs and fit with other goals?
- T = timely: what's my timeline for accomplishing this task?

Being SMART will help you to better understand your goals and so help you attain them. Being SMART is needed not just for success in college, but for career success as well.

A QUICK GUIDE TO TIME MANAGEMENT

- *Keep a calendar and use it—you must schedule specific times for specific tasks (to-do lists are useful, especially in the short-term, but are not sufficient).*
- *Determine and regularly revisit your priorities. Ask what tasks are* urgent *(requiring immediate attention) and what ones are* important *(you need to do them but not immediately). Ask what ones are unnecessary or time-wasters. This is sometimes called "attention management."*
- *For each task, begin by deciding what you want to achieve—be sure that your expectation is realistic ("I'll learn everything about the Bill of Rights in 20 minutes" is not realistic). At the end, ask if you were successful.*
- *Schedule up to three hours of out-of-class study time for every hour you are in class. Some people may need more time than others, and some classes may require a greater investment than others.*
- *Know your style. Do you study more effectively in big blocks of time or in smaller chunks (we explore this further in Chapter Six)? Oftentimes you can more readily reach a big goal if you break it into smaller steps.*
- *Don't insist on 100% perfection—it's better to get something done (hopefully decent!) than nothing.*
- *Don't procrastinate! Often the biggest challenge is to* get going *rather than* keep going.
- *Cramming seldom works in college—for both exams and papers.*
- *Rely on like-minded friends to keep you on track in functional study groups.*
- *Protect your time—don't be easily distracted (for example, turn off social media).*
- *Make time to do other things, such as hang-out with friends and exercise.*

WORKSHEET 3
READ: EFFECTIVE TIME MANAGEMENT

1. Can you really multitask? Perhaps you can, but *how well* do you carry out multiple tasks at the same time? Being able to do something isn't the same as doing it well. Write a paragraph below describing an occasion when you multitasked. How many tasks, what were they, and did you complete them well?

2. How many times in the last two days were you late for an appointment, a class, a date?

3. If you were not late, bravo. Give a few reasons why you think you were not late. What strategies did you use to make sure that you were on time? If you were late, list some reasons why you were late and how you could have avoided being late.

4. Take some time to list two consequences, a minor one and a major one, that might result from being late to each of the following:

a. An appointment with your instructor

Minor consequence:

Major consequence:

b. An exam

Minor consequence:

Major consequence:

c. An application for a scholarship

Minor consequence:

Major consequence:

Please make and attach a copy of Timetable One from Worksheet One and modify or edit it to reflect your actual timetable during the last week (be honest).

CHAPTER 4

ATTENDANCE IS *NOT* OPTIONAL

Of course no one forced you to go to college. We assume you're here because there's something that really interests you, maybe American history. Or perhaps you are here because you have a particular career in mind, such as being a pediatric neurosurgeon. Different people will have different motivations.

With the decision to attend WSU comes a bill. Mom and Dad may be paying, or perhaps you were awarded a scholarship. Maybe you are a recipient of federal financial aid (a loan that must be repaid with interest; private loans such as through banks, usually cost more). In 2018, student loan debt across the nation sits at almost $1.5 trillion—more than the amount Americans owe on their credit cards. Perhaps you have a part-time job, although we'd advise against taking a job, if possible, until you are settled into college life. For the academic year 2017–2018, estimated yearly costs for first-time full-time WSU students who are Washington residents total around $23,000. For non-residents, the total is around $38,000. And these numbers don't include pocket money.

Here's an observation that many instructors make on a regular basis. The lecture theater is full on the first day of class. We see a sea of eager students who realize, or so we hope, that they will never again be able to concentrate so intensely on learning. A week or so later there are empty seats, and the number of empty seats slowly increases as the semester progresses. Maybe the absent students have withdrawn from the class (simply not going to class does *not* de-enroll you, and special procedures exist for withdrawing from and dropping classes). We check the class roster and find that most students are still enrolled. Maybe the absent students are ill, but it seems unlikely that so many would be sick at the same time.

©Hxdbzxy/Shutterstock.com

Why would you waste your time, money, and perhaps future by not going to class, unless you have a really good reason to be absent?

The main reason for absence is truancy, students making the decision not to attend lectures, discussion groups, and labs. In fact, an international survey of college faculty found that students skipping class is the fourth biggest challenge to teaching (the Number One challenge was lack of student engagement when in class). We don't understand this, and we hope you don't either. WSU students are here because they want to be and it is costing someone a lot of money. Truants deprive themselves of the opportunity to learn and they waste money in the process. Of course, some absences are legitimate. You can't choose when you catch the flu, and a scheduled appointment with your orthodontist may be something that can't be changed. Under those circumstances (and other legitimate ones), your instructors may work with you to play catch-up, especially if provided with prior notification. And you must have a Plan B available, perhaps enabling you to borrow notes from someone else in the class.

But just deciding not to attend? That's different, and it really is upsetting to instructors when a student asks if they missed anything by being absent (often worded as "anything important"). A Canadian poet named Tom Wayman wrote a piece he called "Did I Miss Anything?", and here are verses one and three of his poem that addresses this question (we follow Tom's original text by omitting some punctuation):

> "Nothing. When we realized you weren't here
> we sat with our hands folded on our desks
> in silence, for the full two hours

> Nothing. None of the content of this course
> has value or meaning
> Take as many days off as you like:
> any activities we undertake as a class
> I assure you will not matter either to you or me
> and are without purpose"

Does skipping class matter? Let's reword the question: can skipping class affect your success in college and your competitiveness for whatever you decide to do after graduation? The answer is "yes" on both counts. Responsible students don't skip class.

"Did I Miss Anything?" by Tom Wayman from *Did I Miss Anything? Selected Poems 1973–1993*, Harbour Publishing, 1993, www.harbourpublishing.com

SKIPPING CLASS MAY LOWER YOUR GRADE

There are three possible consequences to your grade from deliberately not attending class—it goes up (least likely), it doesn't change (possible) or it goes down (most likely). What does the evidence show?

Many instructors do not take attendance in their classes—like us, they believe attendance should be based on responsible decisions taken by students. However, in fall 2004 we conducted a study in which we were able to attach numbers of lecture absences to final grades for individuals in a large (500+) nonmajors biology class. Here are our major findings:

- All students who attended every lecture passed the class.
- Average final scores dropped 1.5% for every lecture missed.
- The borderline between adjacent letter grades was between 3% and 4%.

It is better to pass a class than fail it, of course, but a D, which is a passing grade, is not very valuable GPA-wise. A drop in final score of 1.5% per lecture missed doesn't sound like very much in a class with about 40 lectures, but look at our third finding. It might only take two or three absences for the B+ you *could* have earned to become a B, or the pass (D) you *could* have earned to be an F. Clearly, skipping class may lower your grade. And now multiply the effect over a few classes.

The importance of class attendance as a predictor of academic performance in college has also been studied nation-wide, and using a much larger sample of students. The data indicate that class attendance is a better predictor of performance, measured as college GPA, than are high school GPA, SAT scores, and study skills (not that we think you should ignore the latter, of course).

We've shown these data to quite a few students over the years, and most respond with surprise if not shock. However, some students simply don't get it. "Oh, I only skip lectures in classes I don't like." "I only skip lectures in classes outside of my major." "I only skip lectures when I don't like the instructor." "I only skip lectures because I can get PowerPoint slides on the Web." We hope that you find comments like these self-defeating and destructive.

We might add here that we appreciate it can feel uncomfortable to be one of perhaps a hundred or more in a lecture theater. One student once told us that there were more students in one of her classes than in her whole hometown! But you can still be an active participant even in a large class. Sit at the front. Answer questions if asked, and ask questions if you find something unclear. It takes courage to do this because you don't want to appear unknowledgeable. But we guarantee that if something is unclear to you then it's unclear to other people as well, so be brave. However, the first thing you must do is to show up.

And perhaps we should end by saying that you should always show up to exams-that's a no-brainer, surely! But perhaps we shouldn't be so certain. In spring 2018 we noticed a missing exam score for a student in one of our 400-level classes (you met her earlier in Chapter 2). We wrote to the student, worried that we had misplaced her score. But we had not. She told us, "I actually missed the first exam. I overslept that day and didn't make it in."

SKIPPING CLASS MAY REDUCE YOUR CUMULATIVE GPA

When you graduate, you will do so with a number that is extremely important in terms of what happens next. This is your cumulative GPA, and it will be carefully considered by a would-be employer or the admissions officer of a medical, law, or graduate school. The individual letter grades that you earn for every class you take contribute to your cumulative GPA (as we discuss in detail later). That's every class you take, not just the classes you like, or the ones in your major, or the ones with pleasant instructors. Why would you risk lowering your cumulative GPA by skipping lectures in *any* of your classes, especially when today's world is so very competitive? Take a look at the following cumulative GPAs required by professional and graduate schools, and you can see why it makes no sense to risk lowering your own:

- Average for medical school: 3.7 out of 4.
- Average for dental school: 3.5.
- Range for law school: 3.0–4.
- Minimum for most Graduate Schools: 3.0.

We should add here that your cumulative GPA is important even before graduation. For example, it will be scrutinized if you apply for scholarships, which provide you with financial support and also help you develop a more impressive resume. It may also need to be above a minimum in order to certify into certain majors (although 2.5 seems to be a typical minimum at WSU, the higher your GPA the more competitive you will be should open slots be limited).

SKIPPING CLASS MAY REDUCE YOUR SKILLS SET

Attending lectures, discussion groups, and labs obviously provides you with the facts and figures important in your classes. Attendance also enables you to develop higher-order cognitive skills such as integration of information (more on such skills later). And it gives you the opportunity to develop what are known as soft, or transferable, skills.

The word "soft" might suggest that something is fluffy and not very important, but nothing could be further from the truth. We prefer the term "transferable skills," because these skills cut across all academic disciplines and all career paths. In fact, we'd go as far as to call them "life skills," and they are in high demand by employers. Following are the kinds of transferable skills, surveyed in 2015, that employers said they wanted to see on applicants' resumes:

- Leadership: 78% of respondents wanted to see evidence of this.
- Ability to work in a team: 78%.
- Written communication skills: 73%.
- Verbal communication skills: 67%.
- Interpersonal skills ("plays well with others"): 61%.

Required by almost 100% of employers were skills such as critical thinking and the curiosity needed to keep learning throughout life. A recent study by Forbes Magazine, which reports on business and finance, found that only about 27% of college graduates work in a job directly related to their major. And so having those transferable skills may well matter more than whether you are a musician or a microbiologist major-wise.

There's a very clear message here—a good GPA simply isn't enough these days, and going to class gives you the opportunity to sharpen your transferable skills. But there's a twist. A survey-based study published in 2018 asked both employers and students how well prepared they thought they were in terms of a range of transferable skills. The results show a huge mismatch between the levels of student proficiency reported by both parties. Here are just two examples. Whereas 79% of

©Hxdbzxy/Shutterstock.com

Don't surf the Web during class, obviously. And, less obviously, don't take notes on your laptop. Hand-written notes result in better learning.

student respondents reported that they were proficient in terms of oral and written communication, only 42% of the employer respondents agreed. And with regard to problem-solving skills, 80% of students reported they were proficient compared to 56% of employers. You might not be as prepared as you think.

CREDIT FOR JUST BEING THERE

It has been suggested that one way to encourage attendance is to offer credit just for being in class. This credit could be built into the grading system for the course or could be in addition to the scores given for compulsory assignments. We are not supporters of providing extra credit of any kind and for any reason, and we believe that incentives for attendance are already in place. First, you get the opportunity to learn about what interests you, and second, you earn a better grade and acquire important skills. And know that your employer will not give you extra credit for "just being there"—turning up for work is taken for granted as simply part of your job. And of course, be engaged when you're in class. We saw a cartoon once (we can't remember where) in which a student complains that, although she attended every class period, her grade wasn't an A. The punch-line, and we paraphrase, was that A doesn't stand for attendance. Being there is just the beginning.

WHAT ABOUT ADVANCED PLACEMENT CLASSES?

For the high school class of 2017, almost 1.2 million students took at least one Advanced Placement (AP) class—a smaller number earned a score of 3 or higher in their AP exams. AP classes taken in high school are popular largely because an AP class with a good score can replace the equivalent class(es) at WSU. Potentially this can save you time and money. The minimum AP score required to obtain WSU credit is 3 out of 5, although some classes require higher scores. For example, as we write this in spring 2018 an AP score of 5 for Calculus AB results in a waiver of the requirement that you take two semesters (eight credits) of introductory calculus required for engineering and certain science majors. To learn more about AP credits (and International Baccalaureate, Cambridge Exams, and CLEP, too), go to www.admission.wsu.edu/apply/ap-ib-and-running-start.

We are a little wary of accepting AP classes too readily, at least in the sciences that we know best. We've seen on a number of occasions that students who took AP Biology weren't as prepared for upper-division courses as were students who took our two-semester sequence of introductory biology. And so, here's our suggestion if you have AP credit. Quietly sit in on the equivalent WSU class in your first or maybe second semester—don't formally register for the class, just sit in the back of the room. If all you see and hear sounds familiar, then the odds are good that your AP class provided a sufficient foundation for later college classes. But if the breadth or depth of material in the WSU class is unfamiliar, we suggest taking that class in the next semester, treating your AP version as an introduction that may help you to earn a better grade. We should stress here that our experience is limited to certain science AP classes and that not all instructors will agree with our position. As is almost always the case, check with an academic advisor if in doubt.

WHY SHOULD YOU CARE ABOUT UNIVERSITY CORE REQUIREMENTS?

The philosophy underlying what are known as the liberal arts goes back to the Ancient Greeks, and an education in the liberal arts was then, and is now, intended to produce an individual able to participate fully as a citizen in a free society. Undergraduate programs in the United States require students to take classes outside of their major in order to become better citizens. Such classes go by many names, such as Distribution Requirements and General Education Requirements. Here at WSU they are known as University Core Requirements, or UCORE classes. We won't go into the details here—you can find a nice discussion of what you'll need to do to satisfy the 12 categories of UCORE at www.ugr.wsu.edu/students/categoriesandcourses.html.

Programs such as UCORE are designed to educate students to become not just better citizens of the United States, but also better and more informed citizens of the world. UCORE classes expose you to the incredible diversities of ideas and peoples that existed in the past and which exist today. They provide you with opportunities to sharpen those important transferable skills that we discussed earlier—the arts and humanities offer opportunities similar to what the sciences offer to become a critical thinker. UCORE classes foster communication and quantitative skills, as well as information

"I have really gotten into
this Roman History course."

©Cartoonresource/Shutterstock.com

literacy (being able to find and evaluate high-quality material). And they also give you a taste of the kinds of areas of study that you might explore if you aren't sure what major interests you the most. UCORE courses are seen by some students as nuisance hurdles to be jumped. We want you to see them as exciting opportunities to explore further the world you live in.

There's another reason why UCORE classes matter, even if you don't like them and don't think they are useful (but you should and they are). As we discussed earlier, all of the courses you take contribute to the GPA with which you graduate—your cumulative GPA, seen by people who are the next link in developing your career. UCORE classes matter to your GPA just as much as the classes you take in your major, so please don't treat them lightly.

We'll end this section with just a few words about WSU's Honors College. For higher-achieving students interested in joining the Honors College, go to www.honors.wsu.edu. Among much else, the Honors College has its own UCORE-type classes, although they are different from and more challenging than the ones taken by non-Honors students. In addition, all Honors students are required to do research and write a thesis based on that work.

SUMMER CLASSES

Classes available during the spring and/or fall semesters may also be offered in the summer. Rather than meeting two or three times per week over 15 weeks, summer classes meet more frequently over a shorter overall period. For example, one of us teaches a summer class that meets every weekday for 75 minutes over six weeks. Taking summer classes isn't for everyone, of course; you may have an internship over the summer, or perhaps you work in order to defray the cost of tuition. In our experience, there are four major reasons why students take classes over the summer:

- Summer classes are often smaller, and involve more one-on-one interaction with other students and the instructor.
- The compressed timeline of summer classes provides an opportunity to really focus tightly on a subject, perhaps a difficult one.
- Students who were short of a few credits and so couldn't graduate in May take (or retake) a class or two to make up the deficit, and so achieve the 120-credit minimum necessary for graduation (40 credits of which must be at the 300- and 400-levels).
- Academically deficient students take classes to boost their GPAs to above the minimum of 2.0 required for reinstatement.

All of these are good reasons for taking classes in the summer. But our advice is to take at least a bit of a break from academics in the summer, if you can. Recharge your batteries so that you are ready to succeed in the fall.

WHAT ABOUT SEMINARS AND PUBLIC TALKS?

One advantage of attending a large research university like WSU is that you are exposed to lots of visitors who come to speak to us about the work they do. It may be scientific research. It may be something creative, such as a reading of fictional literature or a musical performance. Or it might be something such as political or economic action, say on behalf of low-income or minority populations. Take advantage of the opportunity that is provided. Learn more about your interests and maybe think outside the box a little.

A QUICK GUIDE TO LECTURES

- *First of all, plan to go to every lecture (and discussion groups and labs and everything else).*
- *Read relevant lecture material beforehand.*
- *Get there early and sit toward the front.*
- *Don't take lecture notes on your computer—writing them by hand aids learning.*
- *Review your notes soon after a lecture—perhaps even rewrite them.*
- *Use the "double page" method of taking notes (one page for your lecture notes, the opposite page for notes from your textbook and other sources).*
- *Explore other note-taking strategies that may work better for you, such as the Cornell method (Google it).*
- *Develop a logical short-hand, including abbreviations and symbols.*
- *Listen to the instructor and look for clues about what's most important (e.g., a raised voice, repetition, and extra enthusiasm).*
- *Practice listening and writing at the same time.*
- *Compare your notes with those of a friend. Did you each hear the same message?*
- *PowerPoints and other material posted electronically can lead to a very false sense of security. They are not a replacement for class attendance and note-taking.*
- *Participate, be engaged—ask questions and shout out answers. You'll learn more and your instructor will appreciate your enthusiasm.*
- *Ask the instructor if you can record his or her lectures. Respect your instructor's response if it is "Sorry, no."*
- *Have a plan just in case you miss class. Find a friend from whom you can borrow notes. Go to the instructor's office during office hours.*
- *Never ever ask your instructor "Is this important?" or "Will this be on the test?" Everything is important and everything could be on the test.*

"Have fun at school.
Don't hibernate during class."

©Cartoonresource/Shutterstock.com

WORKSHEET 4
READ: ATTENDANCE IS *NOT* AN OPTION

One thing that all college students and college graduates have in common is having missed one or a few classes, not due to unavoidable issues like sickness or emergencies. That's not OK, because persistent lack of attendance for no good reason is not conducive to success and may even be habit-forming. Given tuition costs right now, missing one lecture in a class costs the equivalent of a few days of Starbucks coffee. Why would you waste, *and consistently waste*, money, as well as time?

1. Give five reasons or excuses that you have used to NOT attend class. Don't include unavoidable absences due to sickness or emergencies.

   a.

   b.

   c.

   d.

   e.

2. Take a moment and reflect upon your list. Are you embarrassed or ashamed? Even if you skipped class because the instructor was a horrible teacher (in your opinion), you enrolled, you or someone you know paid your tuition, and so you are breaking your own "contract." Take each of the five reasons or excuses above, and write at least one strategy or rationale that you could use in the future to motivate you to attend every class.

a.

b.

c.

d.

e.

> **Please make and attach a copy of Timetable One from Worksheet One and modify or edit it to reflect your actual timetable during the last week (be honest).**

CHAPTER 5
THE CHANGING FACE OF
FACE-TO-FACE INSTRUCTION

There are many different teaching methods available to instructors, and choosing one is very important because what works best in one context may not work as well in others. Some methods may be better suited to certain subjects than others, or to small rather than larger class sizes. Lectures have been the primary mode of college instruction for who-knows-how-long. Students sit in a big lecture theater, perhaps with as many as 500 or so seats, listening to and taking notes from the instructor standing at the front. Questions are allowed, of course, but most of what is said comes from the instructor, sometimes called a "sage on the stage." It is easy for students to become disengaged in such a setting, to the extent that some fall asleep. We like this quote from the British poet W.H. Auden: "A professor is someone who talks in someone else's sleep." This is sometimes referred to as a Teacher-Centered Approach to Learning, or TCAL.

FROM TCAL TO SCAL

Most of the large classes you take as a first-year student at WSU, both UCORE classes and those in your intended major, will follow a lecture format. Especially, but not only, for large classes, instructors realize that students may feel disconnected, and so we encourage them to become more active participants. Perhaps the instructor shouts out questions in the expectation that students will shout out answers. Another strategy is to cluster students into small groups and have them discuss a question before answering. This is referred to as a Student-Centered Approach to Learning, or SCAL. The majority view is that SCAL results in better learning than TCAL.

A higher-tech way of encouraging active participation by students is through the use of "clickers," small hand-held devices that wirelessly deliver students' answers to a question. A computer records each student's response, and the responses of the whole class can be displayed on a screen. Both students and instructor receive immediate feedback on how well a particular topic is understood.

Another SCAL innovation in teaching is known as the "flipped" classroom. The idea is that, before class, students complete specific readings and, perhaps, watch a mini-lecture provided online by the instructor. Then during class, time can be devoted to problem-solving and active discussion of what the students learned on their own. The "sage on the stage" becomes more of a "guide on the side." This SCAL requires far more effort from students (which might make a flipped class a bit unpopular, at least at first), but there is some evidence that it improves performance in terms of grades, at least in the short term. Flipping is difficult but not impossible with large classes, and we suspect that you will be most likely to encounter flipped classrooms in smaller, upper-division classes in your major.

It is now almost the norm that instructors post class materials online. Here at WSU many instructors put syllabi, lecture outlines, copies of PowerPoint slides, and other materials on a learning management system known as Blackboard Learn. Use this resource, because a recent study found that learning management systems like Blackboard can increase the odds that freshmen become sophomores. Some instructors even post video recordings of their lectures. The upside of this approach is that students have access to relevant material 24/7, and can pace themselves according to their own preferences for when, where, and even how they learn. The downside is that many students think that the online material is all they need. We are quite certain (no, 100% certain) that material posted online unintentionally encourages some students to stop attending lectures.

We think that students miss a great deal by relying largely if not solely on material posted online. Instructors sometimes change their lectures shortly before delivering them. Discussions may arise in class that absentee students obviously miss. And it isn't always clear just how important a certain topic might be without hearing the voice and seeing the body language of the instructor. We encourage students to use online material sensibly, which means seeing it as a supplement to rather than a replacement for face-to-face instruction.

©Corepics VOF/Shutterstock.com

Computers are of increasing importance when taking on-campus classes. They are obviously crucial for classes that are offered online, but you must shut down sites, such as Instagram and Facebook, that might distract you.

There's another way in which technology is impacting how instructors teach and so how you learn. A growing number of classes are available online, enabling you to watch lectures and complete assignments electronically and sometimes according to your own timeline. We don't think it is very likely that you'll take online classes in your first year, but they may become part of your program of study a little later, as might hybrid classes, which combine on-campus and online components. For an overview of so-called "e-learning" at WSU, and all the classes available, and certificates and degrees that can be earned, check out the WSU Global Campus at www.globalcampus.wsu.edu.

The bottom line is that the delivery of class material will be varied and diverse over the time you are in college. Your job is to adapt to these different delivery methods, and to the different teaching styles and personalities of your instructors. Not every one of your instructors will be an exciting speaker who easily catches and then holds your attention. Some subjects you study will catch and then hold your interest less than others, but you must apply yourself regardless if only because every grade you earn will contribute to your cumulative GPA. Adaptability in how you learn is a crucial transferable skill for success in college and beyond.

A WORD OR TWO ON TEXTBOOKS

There seems to be some disagreement in the media about how much students spend on textbooks and other course-related materials, but we recently read that a first-year student might spend around $1,000. We understand that this is a lot of money, and we'll say just two things here, appreciating that textbook cost is a really big "higher ed" issue right now.

First, understand that your instructors require or recommend textbooks and other materials because they believe they are important to your success (so be very sure to use them if you buy them). You can check out sites such as BN.com, Amazon.com, and Half.com to see if used copies are available. Second, understand that we do appreciate that books are expensive and we do try to keep costs down. Some textbooks are available for free as so-called "open source" books—they cost you nothing if used on-line. There are options available that can help lower the cost, such as digital versions of textbooks that you can lease for less than the cost of a print version. You may be able to rent some textbooks. You can team up with a friend or two and split the price. And do remember that we have excellent libraries on campus. You may have the opportunity to sell your book(s) back to The Bookie once a class is finished, but here's a word of advice—even if you have the opportunity, don't sell books that are relevant to your strongest interests. They're the ones to be certain to keep on your shelf.

A WORD OR TWO ON COMPUTERS

It's hard to imagine doing *anything* these days without computers, and that includes studying. Here are a few suggestions for using computers wisely:

- Don't open too many windows all at once. This can encourage multi-tasking, which you almost certainly aren't as good at as you might think.
- It's better to read on paper rather than on screen, because the latter can encourage superficial skimming.
- Taking notes on your computer isn't much more than taking dictation. It makes it hard for you to sift and sort the information when you're busy trying to record everything word-for-word.
- Be kind to your neighbors—they might find your Web surfing to be rather distracting.

In addition, use on-line resources posted by your instructors to best effect. Here's something we recommend very, *very* strongly. If your instructor posts PowerPoint slides on Blackboard, print them three to a page and bring copies to class. Then you can make notes next to the slides as the lecture progresses. Printer paper and toner are among the smallest of your expenses while in college, and for a modest cost you can develop your own customized textbook.

"Can I get full price for these since I never opened them before I flunked out?"

©Cartoonresource/Shutterstock.com

YOUR NAME:

REVIEWER'S NAME:

WORKSHEET 5
READ: THE CHANGING FACE OF FACE-TO-FACE INSTRUCTION

You may have heard about active learning and flipping the classroom. Many of these strategies have been around for a long time, but maybe in different formats, and their recent notoriety should be more accurately described as a resurgence in their use.

The sole purpose of these methods is to engage you, challenge you, and to increase the quality of your classes' learning outcomes. But why should you care? Well, students tend to like consistency in how their courses are taught, but you likely will be exposed to a variety of styles of delivery of course content. You must adapt, or possibly fail.

1. Identify at least three different teaching methods/styles that you have been exposed to in your classes so far. For each one, write a short paragraph stating what you liked about the strategy and what you didn't like. If you have not been exposed to three different teaching methods/styles at the university level, write about the different methods that you were exposed to in high school or community college.

    a.

    b.

    c.

2. You decide on a career as a college teacher. Write two paragraphs on a teaching methodology that you might use in your classes. This methodology must be different from the three discussed above so you may have to do some research on this—maybe talk to your peers or juniors/seniors who are talking different classes, and it must be realistic for use in a university class.

Please make and attach a copy of Timetable One from Worksheet One and modify or edit it to reflect your actual timetable during the last week (be honest).

CHAPTER 6

STUDY SMART *AND* STUDY HARD—LESSONS FROM COGNITIVE PSYCHOLOGY

A serious student doesn't just ask "*What* should I study?", he or she also asks "*How* should I study?" You've probably heard the saying "study smart, not hard" (we Googled it and got nearly 18 million hits!). Our advice when someone asks "How should I study?" is to study both smart *and* hard—they aren't alternative options.

Finding information has never been easier for college students or anyone else (we'll postpone dealing with the issue of the reliability of information until Chapter 8). Here's a very incomplete list of available resources, some more reliable than others:

- Class lectures, discussion and study groups, etc.
- Textbooks (often associated with online tools)
- Bricks-and-mortar libraries
- Khan Academy
- Wikipedia
- TED talks
- YouTube
- Podcasts
- MOOCs
- Google

Psychologists have long known that people find it harder to choose when provided with more choices, but let's assume that you've amassed a good quantity of good quality information (and remember that quantity and quality don't always coincide). How should you study it?

There's a myth believed by many students, especially those in their first year, that learning in college is, or should be, quick and easy. When asked, they'll tell you that learning was pretty easy in high school because they earned good grades. And so, if you think that your first year in college is an extension of high school (what we've called 13th grade), why change your habits? After all, why wouldn't what worked in high school also work in college?

It seems intuitive that instructors should make it easy for students to learn, and that the best strategies for learning by students should be the most straightforward. One of us used to be pleased when student evaluations of his classes said things like "He makes it easy to learn." Why make it harder than it needs to be? As we'll see shortly, intuition can be misleading.

Cognitive psychologists study how we think and how we learn. Most basically, the process of learning can be divided into a number of stages:

- Acquisition of information via the five senses.
- Retention (storage) of information.
- Recall or retrieval (remembering) of information.
- Use of information, perhaps to answer an exam question or, more interestingly and importantly, solve a novel problem.

Drs Robert and Elizabeth Bjork are cognitive psychologists at UCLA, and their careers have been built around the idea that understanding the psychology of how we learn in the research lab should inform how we learn in the lecture theater, library or our dorm room. The most surprising of their findings, all based on careful experiments, is that long-term learning is less effective if the learning strategies we use are too easy. Counterintuitively, there's a level of what they call "desirable difficulty" that leads to better retention of information over longer periods of time. And they make a distinction between performance and learning. "Performance" is your score on a test, so often based on short-term memorization (and which is often over-emphasized in high school, and in some college classes, too). "Learning" is a measure of your deeper understanding of the relevant material, and your ability to use that understanding in a longer time-frame (say, from 100-level classes through upper-division classes and beyond).

Let's review some learning strategies that you should use in your classes that come from studies by cognitive psychologists such as the Bjorks. While these are well known and well discussed in the professional literature, many haven't yet made it very far into the how-to-study college guides.

VARY THE CONDITIONS UNDER WHICH YOU STUDY

While the typical how-to-study guide book tells you to find a single comfy place in which to do your work, the scientific evidence says just the opposite. Efficient long-term learning is improved if you vary the conditions under or in which you study, with minimal distractions. So, tonight use your dorm room. Tomorrow find a quiet spot in the Palouse Study Lounge in the Terrell Library. The next day find a quiet spot in the CUB. Then try a quiet spot in Café Moro. Experiment to determine where it works best for you.

SPACE OUT THE TIMES WHEN YOU STUDY—DON'T BLOCK

You might think that squeezing your study sessions into a big time block helps you learn better than spreading them out into more time blocks but each a bit shorter in duration. Let's say you could choose between studying Chinese opera for four hours on each of two days before an exam versus two hours on each of four days before. The total amount of time spent studying wouldn't differ, but the distribution of that time would. The two options look like this:

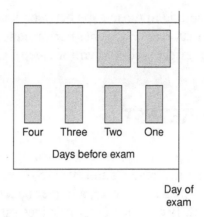

Spacing out your study periods rather than blocking them will lead to better long-term retention and recall. Think about it—in the extreme, blocking is cramming, and students learn pretty quickly that cramming tends not to work well in college. So take your time—study often but in a spaced-out fashion. Don't block it all up. Of course, spacing would mean starting to prepare for an exam a fair time in advance, rather than a day or two before, and that means managing your time effectively.

DON'T STUDY JUST ONE THING FOR LONG PERIODS—INTERLEAF

This sounds rather peculiar. Imagine you have to study three subjects in a biology class—evolution, inheritance, and DNA, abbreviated to E, I, and D. You can study each one on two occasions. You might think that blocking the subjects would be best in terms of long-term learning—do E first, then I, and then D last. But the evidence says otherwise. Your long-term learning of all three subjects will be best if you jumble them up. So, over six learning sessions, you could study E, E, I, I, D, D, which is blocking. Or, you could order them something like E, I, D, I, E, D, which is jumbling:

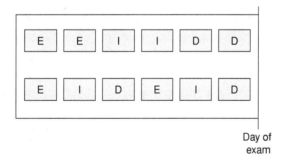

You can see that your overall study effort for each subject is the same. What differs is the distribution of that effort over time, not the total amount. And jumbling things up—or interleaving, to use the technical term—results in the best long-term learning. For cognitive psychologists, this kind of interleaving is an example of what is called "contextual interference." The word "interference" suggests that interleafing should be bad for long-term learning, but scientific evidence shows just the opposite. Students often perceive this as confusion, and the data indicate that a little confusion is a desirable difficulty.

There are two things you should include in those gaps between study sessions—exercise and sleep. A recent study suggests that these may result in higher performance because they allow a more efficient consolidation of memory (an effect well-known for sleep). Our advice—study, go to the Rec Center, and then take a nap.

TEST, RETEST, AND RE-RETEST

There's nothing wrong with rereading your notes and rewriting or redrawing to summarize them. There's nothing wrong with reading and rereading and even re-rereading your text book and what your instructor may have put on a class website. However, a bigger benefit in terms of effective long-term learning comes from testing yourself. If your instructor provides sample questions, answer them. Use the end-of-chapter questions in your text book. All of this takes a certain amount of courage because you might just find you know less than you thought you knew. But there's very good evidence that taking practice tests results in better learning than re-reading, especially under stressful conditions.

What if your answers are incorrect when you test yourself? That sounds like you've learned nothing—well, nothing correct or, even worse, maybe you've learned something that's wrong. The scientific evidence indicates otherwise. You don't have to do well on a practice exam to do well on the real thing. In fact, a student who does poorly on a practice exam, and then researches the correct answers, may do better on the real exam than a student who never even tried a practice exam. When students are given practice exam questions, they often want the answers. The policy on giving answers to practice questions will vary with the instructor, but often answers will not be immediately given. The reason is to make sure that practice questions have value, and that they are used as study guides and for group study. This is all associated with active learning and desirable difficulty. If after studying and actively researching the answers students are still unsure, that's the time to approach the instructor to discuss the correct answer. It is also an opportunity to meet with your instructor during the office hours that are set aside for student meetings. The evidence suggests that trying matters—it isn't just about being correct. You still learn even when you are wrong.

Research shows that study groups are most effective when they are small in size, and involve people who know each other well and share similar learning strategies. Fiercely question the members of your study group—be persistent in getting satisfactory answers (that's what we mean when we talk about a "functional study group"). The scientific evidence is clear—tests aid retention and long-term learning. Simply reading, no matter how many times, is not sufficient if exam success is your goal.

"I GOT THE WRONG ANSWER—I'M DOOMED TO A POOR GRADE"

We've all heard the old saying that you can learn from your mistakes, and it's true. Careful instructors pose you with questions in practice and real exams that don't just determine what you *do* know, but help you determine what you *don't* know so you can ask why. Can you see the twist here? The twist is most obvious in multiple-choice questions. Try this strategy. First, read the question and come up with your best answer without looking at the options provided. Does your answer match one of the options when you do look? A match is a good sign. Here's a second strategy—don't just choose what you think is the *correct* option, but ask why you think the other options are likely to be *incorrect*. Ask not only why you are right but also why you could be wrong. In this way you can learn far more than you would otherwise. Don't see tests as only for assessing what you know. Use them as learning tools as well. Many instructors insist that students wait for a period of time after the exam before sending a query about an exam question. This is principally to encourage you to be thoughtful about your answer, and to encourage you to figure out why your answer was wrong. After careful thought and reflection, often students experience "the penny drops" phenomenon or the "aha"moment—this 'ahah' moment is a much more effective learning strategy than asking the instructor why your answer was wrong. Of course, if you can't figure out why your answer was wrong or you think the question is ambiguous, that is the time to meet with your instructor for clarification. Perhaps the instructor made a mistake—it happens.

Now, we appreciate that learning strategies that employ desirable difficulty are time consuming to use and that there are only 24 hours in a day. Setting priorities (and regularly reviewing them) is crucial to effective time management, as we've said before, and we know that you may not be motivated to adopt a "Bjorkian" approach in every class you take. You might argue that the long-term learning provided by desirable difficulty is not a priority in your UCORE classes (not that we'd agree with you). But hopefully you can see that desirable difficulty is well worth the effort at least for classes in your major, where long-term learning is of greatest importance.

"LET'S JUST GET IT DONE!"

Before he retired as an economist from Princeton University, Dr Daniel Kahneman researched how human beings make decisions. His work suggests that we use two kinds of decision-making strategies, depending on context. When we think fast we tend to be intuitive and emotional, but when we think more slowly we are more likely to be deliberative and logical (the title of his most recent book is *Thinking, Fast and Slow*). Some things need to be thought about so fast that you aren't even aware that you're thinking. Careful and plodding calculations on momentum and acceleration don't make much sense if a hungry cougar is chasing you! But thinking with the goal of learning is best done slowly, even though it requires more mental effort. Most of us would rather not make thinking any harder than necessary, but those desirable difficulties that require careful and critical thinking are slow out of necessity—you can't rush things if your goal is to obtain deep and long-term learning. This idea of a two-level way of thinking is formally known as the Dual Process theory. It reminds us of Aesop's fable in which the slow tortoise ultimately wins out over the faster hare.

There's another context worth mentioning in which Dr Kahneman's distinction seems to have value. When you start college you are a prime victim (victim is the right word, we think) for companies that want you to use their credit cards, potentially getting yourself into a level of debt that could affect your financial status for years into the future. Fast thinking might lead you to go for short-term cash benefits without consideration of longer-term loan costs (that Spring Break in Fort Lauderdale looks mighty appealing, for example). When it comes to financial matters, as well as academic ones, try to be a tortoise rather than a hare.

"I'M JUST NOT 'WIRED UP' FOR THIS SUBJECT"

"I'm just not a math person—I just don't have the 'numbers gene.'" We've heard lots of students say things like this, but the ability to master a particular subject is influenced greatly by how hard we try, our willingness to persevere or "stick with it." In fact, a recent study of twins found that about

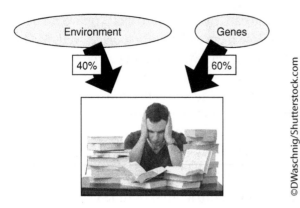

Environment

Genes

40%

60%

©DWaschnig/Shutterstock.com

Close to half of how well we do academically may be due to our environment, which includes study habits, rather than our genes.

40% of the variation in exam scores among a sample of British schoolchildren was due to their environment rather than their genes.

We won't all be Jane Goodall or Felix Hernandez, or Karen Chen or Neil deGrasse Tyson, but the scientific evidence shows that our abilities and talents are fluid rather than fixed. We can improve by trying harder, or, as Stanford psychologist Carol Dweck puts it, by adopting a "growth mindset."

Another thing we hear is along the lines of "I can only learn by listening but not looking." It is true that some of us may prefer to learn by, say, listening rather than looking, but most of us get the best learning experience when we use all of our senses, maybe even at the same time. Again, that's what the science shows (there's actually no evidence that a student does better if taught in what he or she considers his or her "learning style"). When preparing for an exam, try reading aloud from your textbook. Try summarizing important information diagrammatically, perhaps in the form of concept maps (more on them in Chapter 8). You'll be using your eyes, your ears, and the muscles that move your fingers, and you may well learn better as a consequence. This is not to be confused with multitasking, in which you engage in different kinds of activities at the same time, e.g., reading a book and watching Netflix. The evidence there is pretty clear—multitasking lowers performance.

CONNECTING WITH THE MATERIAL: MERRILL'S PRINCIPLES OF TEACHING

Educator Dr M. David Merrill at Utah State University developed what he called the First Principles of Instruction for use by instructors to more firmly connect students with class material. Here we slightly reframe three of Dr Merrill's five principles for your use as a learner:

- The Principle of Activation. When presented with new information, explore how it connects with what you already know—in other words, let new knowledge activate preexisting knowledge. This might involve bringing together different ideas or concepts.
- The Principle of Application. Take what you know and apply it to address a real-world problem. For example, you might ask how a better understanding of the chemistry of photosynthesis in green plants could help us to grow more or better crops.
- The Principle of Integration. Ask yourself how what you are learning fits into your own life and experiences, and with what you do on a day-to-day basis. Maybe you ask how knowing the way muscles work might make you a better weightlifter at the Rec Center. You could go further and discuss integration with your classmates (well, actually you could do that for *everything*).

Placing what you learn into the context of your overall life experiences is an especially powerful learning tool. Notice how all of the principles require you to make an effort in order to connect with the material.

CONNECTING WITH THE MATERIAL: DeWINSTANLEY AND BJORK'S PRINCIPLES OF LECTURING

We've already discussed some of the Bjorks recommendations concerning how you should study to learn most effectively. Together with his colleague Dr Patricia DeWinstanley (at Oberlin College), Dr Robert Bjork has developed a set of guidelines for instructors on how they should teach in order to help students to better learn. Lecturing is just one method of teaching, but it's the one you're likely to encounter the most in your earlier years in college. You'll notice that these guidelines are somewhat parallel to Merrill's Principles of Instruction, and here's our interpretation of them in the form of a diagrammatic summary:

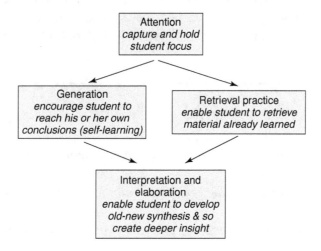

We think it is useful for you to know the ground-plan underlying how your instructors develop and deliver their lectures. A good lecturer first captures and then keeps your attention, perhaps through the careful use of humor and eye-grabbing visual images (but neither of these should be distracting). Next he or she leads you to consider and interpret new material, and recall what you learned previously. And then he or she encourages and guides you to put new and older information together, and so achieve a deeper understanding overall. You will be exposed to a large number of instructors/lecturers/professors with various teaching styles. Depending on how you look at it, this diversity is one of the joys or pains of college, and you will have to adapt to be successful.

Take a few minutes to read the small print in italics and see how these guidelines for instructors can be transformed into guidelines for students to be effective learners. Clearly, you have to make an effort in order to put these guidelines for learning into practice. But by connecting with the material you'll earn better grades in the short term, and achieve a deeper interpretation and retention in the longer term.

THE CHEW OVERVIEW: YOU *MUST* TAKE A LOOK

Dr Stephen Chew is a psychologist at Samford University in Alabama, and he has produced a series of six videos that provides a truly excellent overview of how you as a learner can put into practice discoveries from cognitive psychology such as the ones we discussed above. You can find these videos at www.samford.edu/departments/academic-success-center/how-to-study. We think that everyone should view Dr Chew's videos, and, to whet your appetite, here's a short list of the major points that we take away:

- Effort leads to success, but it must be *effective* effort.
- Basic skills and ideas are a necessary foundation for more complex ones.
- Don't be overconfident—question your understanding often.
- Focus, don't multitask.
- Plan ahead—set goals over different time frames.
- Feedback is good—seek it, accept it, and use it.
- Go to class, pay attention, and use all of the resources available to help you learn.
- Difficulty leads to growth, and failure can lead to learning.
- Find value and relevance in all you do and all you learn.

Dr Chew also has produced a set of five videos that are aimed at showing instructors how applying discoveries from cognitive psychology can make them better teachers. These videos aren't overly technical, and we encourage you to take a look at www.bit.ly/1EGm7fW if you'd like to see what things look like from our side of the fence.

A QUICK GUIDE TO READING YOUR TEXBOOK

- *First of all, commit to reading your textbook!*
- *Psyche yourself for reading—maybe read a newspaper article or two beforehand. Get into the groove.*
- *Once you start reading the text, watch out for "brain fog"—such as rereading and too much underlining.*
- *Preview the text to get an overall impression of its content—look up words you don't know, in a dictionary if necessary.*
- *Then read the text carefully—read to understand and remember.*
- *Don't rush—reading isn't a race.*
- *Make notes, even in the text itself.*
- *Try the double-page method, in which you put notes from your textbook, Google or wherever opposite the notes that you take during class. In this way you produce what is almost a personalized textbook.*
- *Write a précis of what you've read and let a friend read it (a concept map may help—see Chapter 8). Did you capture the important points?*
- *It helps many people to read aloud. Find a quiet space—lock yourself in the bathroom if necessary! Or go and stand in the middle of a Palouse wheat field!*
- *Underlining or highlighting words is not reading and it certainly isn't learning. It might help you remember isolated facts, but that isn't enough.*
- *Use other resources to help you understand, such as reliable websites.*

WORKSHEET 6
READ: STUDY SMART *AND* STUDY HARD—LESSONS FROM COGNITIVE PSYCHOLOGY

The one unassailable fact is that, if you want to be successful in your classes, you must study. (Unless you are in a class that is not challenging, and if that is the case you should speak to your instructor, nicely of course. Alternatively, you are a genius and we are all jealous of your academic prowess). However, most of us need to study in order to get a good understanding of class material, to spend time testing ourselves to determine the depth of our knowledge, and to change our study habits if we are not retaining information and/or if we are not earning the grades we had hoped to earn. As the chapter states there is a lot of research on effective study habits for long-term retention. One size doesn't fit all, and a big part of being a scholar is figuring out what works best for you—knowing what you know or don't know and why (or metacognition). And to add to this complexity is that effective study habits may vary from class to class. You have to recognize that and adapt accordingly.

1. Take a moment to reflect on your own study habits. Pick a class in which you drastically changed your study habits and your midterm or final grade reflected that the change was worthwhile.

   a. Write about the way you studied that was not effective. Give details, and explain why you thought that method of studying would be effective?

   b. What study method did you switch to? Give details. Do you think this method will work for every class you take? Why or why not?

2. Based on this chapter, what new method of study are you *likely* to try? Give details, and explain why you think it might work for you?

3. Based on this chapter, what new method of study are you *unlikely* to try? Give details, and explain why you think it might not work for you?

Please make and attach a copy of Timetable One from Worksheet One and modify or edit it to reflect your actual timetable during the last week (be honest).

CHAPTER 7
THE *ABCD* (AND *F*) OF LETTER GRADES

At WSU, the final grade you earn in a class is a letter grade. Each letter grade is associated with what is known as a grade point as follows:

- F: your grade point is 0 (you failed the class)
- D: 1.0 (you passed, but just barely)
- D+: 1.3
- C−: 1.7
- C: 2.0 (a satisfactory grade)
- C+: 2.3
- B−: 2.7
- B: 3.0 (a good grade)
- B+: 3.3
- A−: 3.7
- A: your grade point is 4.0 (an excellent grade)

That grade point is then multiplied by the number of credits that the class is worth. For example, say you earned a B in Biology 102. The grade point for that grade is 3.0, which we multiply by 4 because the class is worth four credits. Thus the number of earned points for this class is $3 \times 4 = 12$.

Now, let's say you took three courses for a total of 10 credits and 29.9 earned points. (Actually, you probably wouldn't take only 10 credits in a semester, because a 12-credit load is considered full-time for all students, including those with financial aid. Most students aim for 15 credits a semester, but it's important not to overload—remember, the winner is the person who finishes *best*, not *first*.) Your GPA, or grade point average, would be 29.9 divided by 10, which is 2.99 for 10 credits. WSU requires that you complete a minimum of 120 credits in order to graduate (40 of which must be at the 300 and 400 levels). Your cumulative GPA, the one that appears at the bottom of your final transcript, will be the total number of grade points you have earned divided by the sum of all the credits you've taken (including classes that you failed). You cannot graduate with a cumulative GPA below 2.0, and the closer you get to a cumulative GPA of 4.0 the better. A handy online calculator for determining your GPA can be found at www.cougarsuccess.wsu.edu/gpa-calc.

What if your GPA drops below 2.0 before graduation (in 2017, average first-semester GPA was about 2.8)? If either your semester or cumulative GPA drops below 2.0 for the first time, then you will be disenrolled (i.e., dropped from WSU: but simply not going to class *does not* disenroll you) and need to apply for reinstatement. If successfully reinstated, you will then be placed on probation and need to fulfill certain requirements, such as attending workshops on time management and test-taking. If your cumulative GPA drops below 2.0 for three semesters then you will be dismissed from the University. You will have to wait for two academic semesters to pass before applying for reinstatement, which is certainly not guaranteed. This may sound harsh but it truly is in the best interest of a deficient student. It would be far better for that person to better prepare himself or herself for attendance at a four-year school, perhaps by taking classes at a community college, or to reconsider career goals, rather than to continue paying for tuition and potentially waste money and time. We might add here that these grading policies, as well as other academic policies, are nicely summarized at www.catalog.wsu.edu/Catalog/Content/SummaryofAcademicPolicies.pdf.

So here's the big question: what does it take to earn an A at WSU? The simple answer is the obvious one: study hard and study smart. But there's more to it, as you might imagine. Let us explain . . .

BLOOM'S TAXONOMY

Working in the 1950s, Benjamin Bloom was interested in how an understanding of the development of cognitive, or thinking, abilities could translate into specific kinds of learning goals throughout an individual's intellectual development. Although they've been a little revised over the years, Bloom recognized six levels of increasing brain power, or cognitive effort. Taken together, these six levels form what is known as Bloom's Taxonomy. Here's a modern version, slightly different from Bloom's original, shown in the typical pyramid shape:

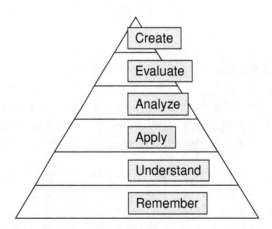

And here are descriptions for the content of each of these six levels, starting at the pyramid's base:
- Level 1: Remember: straightforward recall of relevant information (facts and figures).
- Level 2: Understand: organize, compare, and interpret information.

- Level 3: Apply: use information to solve a novel problem.
- Level 4: Analyze: identify causality and determine generalizations.
- Level 5: Evaluate: judge the truth, quality, and utility of ideas and concepts.
- Level 6: Create: synthesize information to develop a structure or pattern that can be used to solve new problems.

Note how each level requires more cognitive effort than the one below. Thus you can't understand something if you don't remember it. And you can't apply what you know unless you fully understand it. Notice that as you progress upward through the taxonomy you move from mastery of content to mastery of skills, and from mastery of simple memorization to mastery of understanding.

Although some have criticized details of the validity of Bloom's Taxonomy, it guides many instructors in how they teach and how they assess the knowledge of their students. And that means that you, the learner, must appreciate that simply remembering facts and figures often won't be sufficient to earn a good grade. For example, here's a question on America's own music, jazz, that clearly requires nothing more than simple recall, and so is at Level 1 of Bloom's Taxonomy:

> "Who among the following was or is a famous jazz trumpeter?
>
> a. Thelonius Monk
> b. John Coltrane
> c. Elvin Jones
> d. McCoy Tyner
> e. Miles Davis"

Here's a question involving the same individual (Miles Davis) that is closer to Level 5 of Bloom's Taxonomy, and so requires a greater level of cognitive effort:

> "Bebop jazz, a style starting in the 1940s, gave way in part to so-called Cool jazz in the 1950s. Explain how these two styles differ in terms of trumpet playing, using the music of Miles Davis as a case study."

True, these two questions differ in format, the first being multiple-choice and the second requiring an essay as response. But more important is that the second question could not be answered purely on the basis of factual recall. A good answer to the second question requires analysis and evaluation. Among other things, it would discuss how Davis' Bebop tends to be played fast, with rapid chord changes and a high level of improvisation, whereas his Cool jazz is often slower and more melodic ("laid back"), and has a more formal structure.

BLOOM AND GRADES

If Bloom's Taxonomy guides us as instructors in developing our classes and methods of assessment, then you need to know what it takes to earn a particular letter grade. It is true that questions at higher cognitive levels will become more common and so important in your upper-division classes, but you should expect at least some higher-level questions in your 100- and 200-level classes.

As we discussed earlier, WSU uses letter grades, and the grading scheme that is advanced by the Registrar's Office is rooted in Bloom's Taxonomy. Here it is in the format that we use in our upper-division classes:

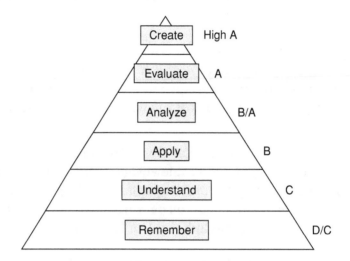

If we add some detail, then the so-called grading rubric looks like this:

- D/C: remembering, or "regurgitation," of facts and figures.
- C: understanding, the ability to summarize, explain, and reword.
- B: application, the ability to use what you know to address or solve a novel problem.
- B/A: analysis, putting data-related facts and/or ideas together to produce an original product.
- A: analysis and evaluation, combining data to produce an original product.
- High A: evaluation and creation, the judgment and rating of ideas in ways that pit them against others, and which creates new knowledge. This is one definition of critical thinking (more on that later).

How will your letter grade be determined? So-called methods of assessment will include, but may not be limited to, exams, quizzes, research papers and, in the sciences, lab reports of some kind. For most students it is exams that are of greatest concern. So, adding to the recommendations given in Chapter Six, how should you prepare for an important exam?

FLASH CARDS AND CONCEPT MAPS

We believe that one of the worst inventions in education is flash cards. Their use is ubiquitous. If we walk through Todd Hall and people are sifting through stacks of flash cards, then we know exactly what those students are waiting for—an exam. But think about it. What can you put on a flash card? It is often a piece of isolated information. There are so many examples we could give. "On what ship did Charles Darwin travel the world?" (the Beagle). "When did the American Civil War begin and end?" (1861 and 1865).

While these are important facts and figures in biology and American history, questions that require them as answers are at the lowest level in Bloom's Taxonomy. Flash cards may be fine for simple recall, but they aren't helpful for understanding, applying, analyzing, evaluating and creating, and comparing and interpreting information. While flash cards have value, they can result in a false sense of security in terms of how well a student understands a concept. Relying on flash cards may earn you D and C grades, but perhaps not much higher.

Imagine that you spread your flash cards across the floor and connect them with arrows. What you've drawn is a concept map. Sometimes called a thinking map, a concept map is a diagrammatic way of summarizing important facts, figures, and concepts or ideas. It also shows how data and ideas are connected to one another so that a bigger picture emerges. Making such connections obviously is of use when studying for an exam, especially when tackling questions that require application, analysis, evaluation, and creation (higher levels in Bloom's Taxonomy). Concept maps also help to organize content when writing a paper or giving an oral presentation, and so sharpen both written and verbal communication skills.

A simple example of a concept map is shown below. We won't go into all of the details of how to construct such maps—one website that we think is especially valuable in this regard is www.cmap.ihmc .us/docs/theory-of-concept-maps.php. However, in brief, the map consists of nodes (shown as boxes) connected with arrows. Nodes contain facts, figures, and concepts or ideas. The arrows indicate relationships among nodes—the arrows may be labeled to show the nature of those relationships. In this simple example, you can see the relationships among the major players (in square nodes) that are involved in teaching and learning at WSU:

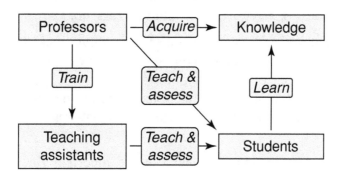

Concept mapping is a skill often taught in high school, but many college students seem to have forgotten the skill or believe that it has no value in college. We couldn't agree less. Concept maps help you connect ideas and, on exams, enable you to better answer questions that are at higher levels in Bloom's Taxonomy. They help you engage in critical thinking, something we'll look at in the next chapter.

WHAT ARE YOU WORKING FOR?

That probably sounds to you like a really silly question because the answer is so obvious—good grades so as to get a good job. Social psychologists recognize two ways in which we are motivated to work toward our goals (and not just academic goals—we could just as readily be talking about sports and hobbies). In academics, *intrinsic motivation* drives us to accomplishment through the personal enjoyment and satisfaction we obtain from learning itself and from meeting a challenge—it is self-driven. *Extrinsic motivation* drives us in the hope that we will gain a reward for doing well, such as praise, money, or a good grade—it comes from outside of ourselves. Research by Dr Mark Lepper and his colleagues at Stanford University has shown that, when someone's motivation switches from intrinsic to extrinsic, their performance can go down. This so-called "overjustification effect" may explain why the inquisitive nature of young children who simply love to learn can become squashed later in life. Then the joy of discovery and learning can be replaced by the reward of pleasing others (parents, instructors) and the punishment of earning poor grades. Good grades are important, of course, but try hard to maintain or relocate that intrinsic love of learning you had in fifth and sixth grade. As instructors we can try to foster the intrinsic motivation of our students through the use of diverse teaching methods (not just one-way lectures), by showing how what we teach and what you learn connects with real life, and by providing timely feedback on papers, exams, and other assessment tools. But you have to meet us half-way, at least.

15 TO FINISH

Before moving on, we need to expand just a little on how large a credit load must be to be considered full-time. As we mentioned earlier, right now 12 credits per semester is considered full-time (for Pell grants, for example). But there's a big push developing nationally to make 15 credits the minimum for being a full-time student. The so-called "15 to Finish" movement promotes the idea that completing 15 credits increases timely graduation rates, but we're not completely convinced right now. One data-set presented as evidence for this comes from Virginia's public four-year colleges. With 15 credits in their first semester, 74% of Virginian students graduated within six years. With 12 to 14.5 credits, that number dropped to 63%. Note that the numbers refer to the *first* semester, not *every* semester, and that the graduation rates are for within *six* years, not *four*.

15 to Finish is not without critics. First, the number of non-traditional students who are enrolled part-time in U.S. colleges is rising fast, and encouraging people who have jobs and perhaps families to enroll in 15 credits may be encouraging them to overload (see Chapter 10). Second, 15 credits may be an overload for students of all types, traditional or not, if they are a little less prepared academically. And third, it may lead students to enroll in classes that aren't useful in their majors just to make "the magic 15."

We acknowledge that timely graduation rates obviously are important. But we also stress here, as we have elsewhere, our opinion that the winner in higher-ed is the person who finishes *best*, not necessarily *first*. Let your academic advisor help guide you in determining the path to degree that best fits your personal circumstances now and your goals for the future.

A QUICK GUIDE TO TAKING EXAMS

PREPARING BEFOREHAND

- *Create a "functional study group"—question one another persistently and mercilessly (but kindly).*
- *Take every opportunity to test your knowledge through every quiz available. You can't test yourself too much.*
- *Read but don't only read.*

- *Take your notes and précis—then précis the précis. But don't only précis.*
- *Use flash cards sparingly, for facts and figures, and use concept mapping liberally to connect ideas.*
- *Cramming seldom works in college—start preparing for a major exam at least one week in advance (assuming you have put in as many as three hours of study before and after each lecture). Interleaf different topics rather than study them in discrete blocks.*
- *Know what kind of exam it is—multiple choice, fill-in-the blanks, essay.*
- *Know what material the exam will cover, e.g., is it comprehensive?*
- *Be curious about why wrong answers are wrong, not just about why correct answers are correct.*

ON THE DAY

- *Be as rested and relaxed as possible, and be neither thirsty nor hungry.*
- *Use ear plugs if you are easily distracted by noise.*
- *Look over the whole exam briefly.*
- *Read each question—understand each question. If you don't understand a question then ask the proctor.*
- *Answer easy questions first.*
- *Multiple choice: try to figure out the correct answer without looking at the options.*
- *Multiple choice: if you don't know the correct answer, try to rule out the wrong ones.*
- *Multiple choice: anticipate questions of the form "Is it a, b, a+b, a+c, none of the above, all of the above." These are valid questions. They aren't trick questions but they can be tricky.*
- *Essays: write an outline first to capture the important points you want to make (perhaps sketch out a concept map).*
- *Essays: write legibly.*
- *Essays: look at the space available and fill it (but only with good text). Writing six sentences on a blank full page certainly won't be adequate, and trying to squeeze a page of text into a paragraph will certainly be too much. Organize your thoughts before you write.*
- *Essays: if the question has multiple parts, underline each so that you can see all of the parts easily as you answer them.*
- *Essays and short answers: write legibly, and remember that good spelling, grammar, and punctuation are important.*
- *Be aware of Bloom's Taxonomy when reading the question and choosing or writing your answer—are you being asked to remember, explain, synthesize, integrate, and/or problem solve?*
- *To the extent possible, take your time (WSU exams are usually timed, so be careful). If you are struggling with a question, move on to the next and return to it later if you have time.*
- *And remember that the winner is the person who finishes best, not first.*

ONCE THE GRADES COME BACK: SOME QUESTIONS TO ASK

- *Did you earn a good grade? Great! A disappointing grade? Don't panic!*
- *If you did well, what was it about how you studied that contributed to your success? Think about this carefully because, obviously, you want to adopt the same strategy again.*
- *If your grade was disappointing, do you think the way you studied may have let you down? What will you do differently in preparing for the next exam? You might discuss your ideas with your instructor and members of your "functional study group."*
- *If there's an answer key use it. For questions you answered poorly, did you simply not know the material, or did you not really understand what you were being asked? For example, did you simply repeat facts and figures, or definitions of concepts, when you should have* used *those concepts, thus showing a deeper level of understanding of the material (that would be answering at a higher level in Bloom's Taxonomy)?*
- *And remember, exams don't just assess what you know but also help you to learn more deeply. It might sound trite, but you truly can learn from your mistakes.*

WORKSHEET 7
READ: THE *ABCD* (AND *F*) OF LETTER GRADES

By this point in the semester you have taken some exams. You may be able to predict what your final grades will be. And you may be able to predict what semester GPA those grades will translate into and what effect your semester GPA will have on your cumulative GPA.

This is a reflective worksheet. According to the WSU Registrar's Office, students must have specific skills in order to earn letter grades A through D. These guidelines are in place to guide instructors on writing exam questions and in the subsequent grading of students' answers.

1. Without using any specific class name (or any identifier), write a paragraph about a class, or an exam in a class, in which you earned an A, and you believe you did not earn that A based on the Registrar's Office guidelines summarized in the chapter. Explain what skills the exam tested and what grade you think you should have been awarded assuming you answered all the questions correctly. In other words, if you feel that the questions required you to memorize content and you got them all correct, then you might have expected to earn a C or D grade. How do you feel about earning this grade—good, bad, delighted, or undeserving? Explain your reasoning, and suggest an action that you should take such that students, in future, are not subjected to this inaccurate grading scheme

2. Without using any specific class name (or any identifier), write a paragraph about a class, or an exam in a class, in which you earned a C, and you believe you did not earn that C based on the Registrar's Office guidelines summarized in the chapter. Explain what skills the exam tested and what grade you think you should have been awarded assuming you answered all the questions correctly. In other words, if you feel that the questions required you to analyze and evaluate and you got them all correct, then you might have expected to earn an A grade. How do you feel about earning this grade? Explain your reasoning, and suggest an action that you should take such that students, in future, are not subjected to this inaccurate grading scheme.

Please make and attach a copy of Timetable One from Worksheet One and modify or edit it to reflect your actual timetable during the last week (be honest).

CHAPTER 8
CRITICAL THINKING IS, WELL, CRITICAL

One of our biggest goals as educators is to help you become critical thinkers. Critical thinking is a bit of a slippery concept. Everyone knows what it is but there's no easy formal definition we can all agree on (and there's no easy agreement on how to help you develop it). For us, critical thinking involves the three highest levels in Bloom's Taxonomy, what we'll call here analysis, evaluation, and creation. Here's what an organization known as the Foundation for Critical Thinking has to say about the abilities developed by a critical thinker (www.criticalthinking.org/pages/defining-critical-thinking/766):

"A well cultivated critical thinker:

- Raises vital questions and problems, formulating them clearly and precisely.
- Gathers and assesses relevant information, using abstract ideas to interpret it effectively.
- Comes to well-reasoned conclusions and solutions, testing them against relevant criteria and standards.
- Thinks open-mindedly within alternative systems of thought, recognizing and assessing, as need be, their assumptions, implications, and practical consequences.
- Communicates effectively with others in figuring out solutions to complex problems.

Critical thinking is, in short, self-directed, self-disciplined, self-monitored, and self-corrective thinking. It presupposes assent to rigorous standards of excellence and mindful command of their use. It entails effective communication and problem-solving abilities and a commitment to overcome our native egocentrism and sociocentrism."

Perhaps all of that sounds a bit long-winded—we'd have to agree. More user-friendly are the results of some research carried out by Dr Michael Hogan, a cognitive psychologist at the National University of Ireland. He has found that, out of 12 "key dispositions" possessed by good critical thinkers, three are particularly important—and you should start cultivating them if you haven't already started:

- Curiosity, a drive to find answers and solve problems.
- Open-mindedness to new ideas and criticism from others.
- Confidence in your own abilities and positions, but not arrogance.

Take a moment to self-reflect on these: do you have them, and if you do, could you improve in any of these areas? Here's a quote from the British philosopher Bertrand Russell: "Most people would sooner die than think, and most of them do." That does sound rather harsh, but it stresses the fact that thinking critically is hard work. We know that it takes a lot of effort for instructors to teach critical thinking (in fact it is not clear that critical thinking *can* be taught) and it is clear that many students have to work hard to think critically. But, and pardon the pun, critical thinking is critical to your *college* success and your subsequent *career* success. Expect to start (continue?) your training as a critical thinker in your first year of college, and then expect to do more and more of it as you move toward being a senior.

THE SCIENTIFIC METHOD AS A MODEL

While this isn't a book for science majors only, there is a model for critical thinking that every college student simply has to know—if you aren't seeing it in any of your current classes then Google it. This model is known as the Scientific Method but, as you'll see, its relevance and value cut across all disciplines.

The Scientific Method begins with an original *observation*—you see something, and perhaps you wonder "why" or "how." Next you come up with a *hypothesis*, which is simply a possible answer to your why or how question. Then, based on previous knowledge, you develop *predictions* that arise from your hypothesis, along the lines of "if answer X is correct, then I'd expect to see Y and Z." You *test* your predictions by making additional observations, perhaps coming from an experiment involving some kind of manipulation. If those additional observations support your hypothesis, then you cautiously accept the latter as the correct answer to your question. If your additional observations don't support your hypothesis, then it's back to the drawing board. Perhaps you revise your original hypothesis, or come up with a new one that makes new predictions that you subject to a new test.

A hypothesis or set of related hypotheses that has been tested and supported time and time again becomes a *theory*, about as close to a proven fact as we get in science. Note that this use of the word theory is just the opposite of its everyday meaning, which is a best guess. For example, our theory in the everyday sense on February 4 2018 was that the New England Patriots would beat the Philadelphia Eagles to win Super Bowl LII. So much for our "theory!" The Eagles won, and the score wasn't even close (41 to 33).

Here's a diagrammatic summary of the basics of the scientific method. Let's illustrate how it works with what might seem to be a rather trivial problem. But it will give you a feel for how the method can be used outside of science.

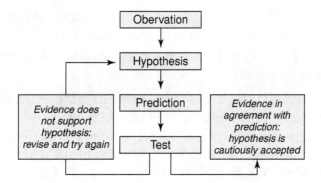

The power goes out in your apartment, you reach for your flashlight, you toggle the switch, and nothing happens. You've made an observation. You ask why your flashlight isn't working. You hypothesize that the batteries are dead. If correct, then you predict that the flashlight should work if you change the old batteries for new ones. You test this prediction by changing the batteries, a kind of mini-experiment. If your flashlight now works then your hypothesis of dead batteries is supported. If it doesn't then you come up with a new hypothesis—maybe you test whether the bulb is broken.

While this seems like a trivial problem, it shows how we use the scientific method in our everyday lives, not just in a science lab. If you really want to know why your flashlight doesn't work, what other approach might you take? Perhaps you'd change the batteries and the bulb at the same time. The flashlight might then work, but you wouldn't know what caused the problem you've just solved. Many non-science students find the scientific method to be rather daunting, but to quote the great physicist Albert Einstein, "The whole of science is nothing more than a refinement of everyday thinking." When was the last time you used a version of the scientific method (hypothesis-prediction-test) to solve an everyday problem or answer an everyday question?

EXTENDING THE MODEL BEYOND EXPERIMENTAL SCIENCE

Now let's employ the logic that underlies the scientific method to think critically about what the vast majority of scientists see as an extremely important issue in today's world. You read that global climate is changing and that the vast majority of scientists say human activity is largely responsible. You could simply take those two statements at face value—after all, scientists are experts and they surely know what they're talking about. That is obviously not a very critical way of thinking about the statement. A critical thinker would ask questions. What evidence do we have that climate is really changing? How reliable is that evidence? For example, have temperature measurements been made in a careful and consistent manner? What evidence do we have that climate change, if reliable evidence indicates that is occurring, is due to human activity? How reliable is that evidence? If we find a human–climate connection, is it merely an association or a real cause–effect relationship? Have alternative explanations been considered (such as solar flares or sunspots), and if so, why have they been dismissed? And if the evidence indicates that human activity is causing global climate change, then how? Deforestation? Burning fossil fuels?

That example is obviously based on science, although not science that is readily amenable to experimental manipulation. Let's try another example that comes from the arts. You read that William Shakespeare may not have written all of the plays that are attributed to him. You could take this at face value—after all, academics who study English literature know a lot more about those plays than most of us. But a critical thinker would ask questions concerning the evidence for such a claim. Is it true that

Shakespeare wasn't sufficiently educated to write so well? Evidence suggests he attended grammar school and had access to books, so the hypothesis of poor education isn't well supported. Is it true that the Earl of Oxford wrote the plays? Perhaps not, or at least not all of them, because the earl died before some of Shakespeare's plays appear to have been written.

Evaluating evidence for global climate change and authorship of the works of Shakespeare may seem like very specialized examples of the importance of critical thinking. But while it is a difficult and time-consuming skill to learn and perfect, we believe that the ability to think critically cuts across all majors and all careers (and remember that it is a transferable skill highly valued by employers). It is as important for a plumber to think critically ("How can I tell if this pipe is leaking due to a bad connection rather than rust?") as it is for a physician to think critically ("What symptoms would I expect to see if this patient has migraine rather than a brain tumor?").

EXTENDING THE MODEL INTO EVERYDAY LIFE

You may have heard the saying "May you live in interesting times" (said to be, but probably not, an old Chinese curse). We are certainly living in an interesting time in the U.S. We do not intend to get all politically-partisan here, but it is simply true that we are continually exposed to a lot of misinformation like never before, and it has perhaps never been more important for us to think critically in order to be informed, thoughtful, and engaged citizens.

In the fall of 2016 a rumor went viral that a U.S. politician was part of a child-sex ring operating out of a pizza parlor in Washington, D.C. No evidence whatsoever was offered to support this astonishing claim, which clearly was a piece of what has become known as "fake news." However, it certainly was thought sufficiently credible by at least one member of the public, who went to investigate the pizza parlor with a firearm that he discharged. And a few years ago, it was proposed—based on no scientific evidence—that the measles-mumps-rubella (MMR) vaccine causes autism in at least some young children. We've all become aware that we may be told "facts" that simply aren't true. Indeed, the Oxford English Dictionary made the term "post-truth" its word of the year for 2016—defined as a case or situation in which objective facts matter less than emotions and feelings. Then in early 2017 we were introduced to the concept of an "alternative truth," in which a lie or a mistake is considered to be just as valid as an objective and verifiable truth—it's just an alternative, no worse and perhaps even better.

We are bombarded with information from when we get up to when we go to bed—through radio, TV, newspapers, Google, Facebook, Twitter, and many other sources. But what information is reliable and what isn't? A recent study out of Stanford University found that younger people, typically considered to be the most tech-savvy among us, are actually pretty bad at separating Web-based news stories from paid promotions. With close-to-complete access to the Web, it has never been easier to spread and be fed (mis)information quickly and cheaply. The ability to tell the difference between fake news and real news, and alternative truths and reals truths, are part of a skill—set called information literacy. It really doesn't much matter to most of us whether supermodel Kendall Jenner (part of the infamous Kardashian clan) has had cosmetic surgery on her face, But it surely matters greatly if belief in fake news potentially could have resulted in someone being shot in a pizza parlor in Washington, D.C. Or that the vaccine-preventable disease of measles has made something of a comeback when, in 2000, it was declared to be eliminated from the U.S. A 2017 measles outbreak in Minnesota resulted in almost 80 confirmed cases and more than 20 hospitalizations. Infection with the virus that causes measles can be fatal, especially (but not only) in the so-called developing world.

Sharpening your skills at critical thinking and information literacy are among the goals underlying WSU's UCORE program. Here are just a few suggestions for help in evaluating what you read, see, and hear:

- Does the source seem to be reliable? What are the credentials of the writer (maybe Google him or her)? A story written by a university professor in the *New York Times* or *Washington Post* has a higher chance of being accurate and correct than one in an obscure blog, or on the front page of a tabloid like the *National Enquirer* at the Walmart checkout. A higher chance may not be 100% certainty, of course.
- Carefully examine the domains of websites. Those ending in .edu are there to inform, hopefully reliably (but always be cautious). Those ending in .com are likely to be trying to sell you something, with no guarantee of reliability at all. A website that is littered with adverts may be more interested in selling than informing.
- Be wary of statements, such as "An anonymous source told us . . ." or "As we all know . . ." or "I think that . . ." The most reliable information will come from a named source whose qualifications are available or checkable.
- If a headline is outrageous or at least unlikely, such as "Beyonce spotted borrowing music CDs from Pullman's Neill Public Library", then beware. We exaggerate a little here to make our point, but even headlines that sound plausible may be fake news.
- In an academic setting, always check if the piece you are reading was reviewed by the author's peers for reliability. Such peer-review is standard practice for academic journals and, while not fool-proof, it helps to assure reliability.
- If a so-called fact sounds weird or suspicious, check it on a fact-checking website such as www.FactCheck.org.

Fake news and information have always been with us, and we must all honestly acknowledge that we may be influenced by our *own* biases (and self-deceptions) just as much as we may be influenced by the biases (and deceptions) of *others*. We could debate whether there's more false information out there these days than before, whether we have more access to it or whether we're just more aware of it. But more important is to bear in mind that a good critical thinker isn't cynical or distrustful, but he or she is skeptical. A skeptic asks questions and is always looking for evidence-based answers. A skeptic follows the advice of an old Russian proverb popularized in the U.S. by President Ronald Reagan: "Trust, but verify."

A BIT ON BIAS AND UNCERTAINTY

A good critical thinker acknowledges the importance of bias in shaping how he or she interprets what he or she sees and hears. Perhaps the political realm is most obvious here, although it certainly isn't unique (the Left and the Right may see the same facts, but interpret and spin them in different ways).

There are lots of ways in which we might be, and often are, biased cognitively (Google "cognitive biases" for more detail), but we'll identify just one here. It's called "confirmation bias," and it occurs when you search for or too readily accept what appears to confirm your prior beliefs or supports your favored hypothesis, without carefully considering alternatives. Try to avoid all biases, but especially confirmation bias. Hopefully you can see the connection between confirmation bias ("I think this *should* be true") and alternative fact ("I think this *must* be true"). (The television satirist Stephen Colbert coined the term "truthiness" for believing that something must be true just because it feels true).

He may not have been the first or only, but Founding Father Ben Franklin is believed to have said that only two things in life are certain—death and taxes. The easiest way to teach is to present facts, figures and, especially, ideas as things that are known and understood with complete certainty. But 100% certainty is much less common than you might think, especially given the right-or-wrong way in which so much is taught in high school (and in some college classes, too). Especially early in their college careers, some students can get frustrated if professors tell them not to always expect black-or-white or right-or-wrong answers. A good critical thinker weighs alternatives, acknowledges his or her own biases (we all have them), and doesn't shun away from uncertainty and ambiguity. In fact, he or she embraces the latter. But beware—that doesn't mean that we should give "alternative facts" equal air-time once we identify them as lies, mistakes or positions not supported by evidence.

YOUR BRAIN IS A MUSCLE—FLEX IT

Muscle cells and brain cells differ in lots of ways, but they are similar in one crucial respect—both improve the more they're used. Just as muscles get stronger with use, so too do brains get better at thinking, and thinking critically. As we said earlier, no one likes to work too hard. But in the same way as physical hard work in the gym grows muscle power and endurance, so intellectual hard work builds brain power. Too many people think that how well they can do (how smart they are) is somehow fixed, perhaps at birth and by your genes, whereas in reality our abilities are far more fluid than most of us imagine, for both muscle and brain. Improvement can come from increased effort. We recommend that you adopt what Stanford psychologist Carol Dweck has called a "growth mindset," in which the more you put in, the more you get out. Rob Jenkins of Georgia State University Perimeter College has written that making an effort even in the classes you like the least and/or making the most effort in the classes you find most difficult is like hardcore cross-training for your brain. We like an analogy based on the brain's anatomy—we envisage cortical cartwheels, limbic leaps, and hippocampal high-jumps as good brain exercises! It takes a lot of brain power to be careful, cautious, cool, critical, fair, objective, and unbiased. As Rob says, what better place to hone these skills than a college classroom.

©Syaheir Azizan/Shutterstock.com

A critical thinker evaluates, remembers, understands, and then uses the knowledge that he or she acquires. Then he or she asks further questions, living as a life-long learner!

A QUICK GUIDE TO WRITING PAPERS

- *Writing is a transferable skill that employers want to see—take it very seriously.*
- *What is the purpose of what you are writing? Is it purely descriptive or argumentative?*
- *Create an outline—start small and work up (from words to sentences to paragraphs).*
- *A concept map can help you connect your ideas with one another* (see Chapter 7).
- *Write the easiest sections first to avoid writer's block. Writing is seldom a linear process, running smoothly from introduction to conclusion, start to finish.*
- *Be sure to introduce your topic early—clearly state your goal, question, or hypothesis.*
- *Provide a summary of your topic and your main points or conclusions at the end of your paper. Bring the reader back to where you started in a conceptual circle.*
- *Do your sentences and paragraphs flow and connect with one another? Again, a concept map can help you do this.*
- *Check for good grammar, punctuation, and spelling. You'll be penalized for poor technical quality in your writing.*
- *If provided with a specific format, use it. Modern Language Association (MLA) style is a common format used in the arts and humanities, but there are others. Ask your instructor if you aren't sure what format to use.*
- *Reread and revise as much as needed, and don't underestimate the importance of this—give yourself plenty of time, because good writing cannot be rushed.*
- *Use your friends—peer-review can be really useful if honest and constructive, and provided by a functional study group.*
- *Visit the Undergraduate Writing Center for help if you need it: www.writingprogram. wsu.edu.*
- *Save your best pieces of graded written work for possible inclusion in your Junior Writing Portfolio (you'll need three pieces of graded work signed by the instructor): www.writingprogram.wsu.edu/university-writing-portfolio.*

WORKSHEET 8
READ: CRITICAL THINKING IS, WELL, CRITICAL

Critical thinking is a much-used term with many different meanings, including: the ability to go beyond class content, to apply content in other contexts, to analyze content weaknesses and strengths, to extend your understanding of content, to evaluate evidence for the content, and/or to propose a different explanatory mechanism or hypothesis.

Critical thinking involves certain skills. Please read the paragraph below and write a brief response to each question assessing a specific skill.

> "Recent data show that about one in 5 students at the start of their first semester will leave WSU at the end of their first year, a number close to the national average. And the data show that only about three or four in 10 students will actually graduate in 2022, four years after the start of their studies the degree. (almost all of our degree programs should, in principle, last no longer than four years). For full-time, first-time college students at public universities, the national average for graduation rates in six years was about 59% for the Class of 2013. By any measure, these are all disappointing numbers."

1. Apply. If you have 98 freshmen friends, how many of you (including yourself) will not return for your sophomore year? Show your work.

2. Analyze. Can you come up with a weakness in the content of the paragraph, a criticism of the data presented?

3. Extend. List three reasons to explain why a student might take six years to graduate from WSU with a degree. For each reason suggest a possible fix.

a.

b.

c.

4. Evaluate. Are the data presented in the paragraph significant? What does significant mean? How could you determine if the data are significant?

5. Propose. Perhaps the retention and six-year graduation rates reported in the paragraph are due, at least in part, to something other than poor transition skills to college. Suggest and explain three plausible alternative explanations for these data.

a.

b.

c.

Please make and attach a copy of Timetable One from Worksheet One and modify or edit it to reflect your actual timetable during the last week (be honest).

CHAPTER 9
SCHOLARS DON'T CHEAT—ACADEMIC INTEGRITY

As a successful college student you are on the road to becoming a scholar, a dedicated expert in your field of study. Scholars don't cheat—they show academic integrity. We'll define cheating as any activity that does or could result in you earning a grade that is inflated due to dishonesty. This sounds pretty straightforward, but it can sometimes be unclear and confusing, as we'll explain.

OVERT AND OBVIOUS

During the exam we see your eyes repeatedly gaze at the paper of the person next to you. This looks like cheating. If we then find that your exam matches that of your neighbor, the evidence that you cheated is strong. (Let's add here that the place where you take your exam, usually the lecture theater, was designed to seat many students, so you are likely to be very close to your neighbors.) Here's another obvious example. You come to the physics exam with formulae written on your hand, which you peek at when you think no one is looking. But you are being watched because, unfortunately, we instructors have plenty of experience with cheating.

©Jaromir Chalabala/Shutterstock.com

> *Do you really think we won't catch you? Is the cost of being caught really worth taking the risk?*

71

If we catch you cheating then we will respond according to both class and University policy. The former will be provided in your syllabus and the latter can be found at www.academicintegrity.wsu.edu. You might receive an F grade for that particular exam or fail the course. Perhaps you will be required to do some form of community service as a penalty. Or maybe you will be dismissed from the University. The penalties can be harsh, but remember, students aspiring to become scholars don't cheat.

MORE SUBTLE AND MORE DANGEROUS

There's another kind of academic dishonesty for which instructors and the University have no tolerance, and that is plagiarism. Here's how the Washington Administrative Code, adopted by WSU, defines plagiarism:

> "Presenting the information, ideas, or phrasing of another person as the student's own work without proper acknowledgment of the source. This includes submitting a commercially prepared paper or research project or submitting for academic credit any work done by someone else. The term 'plagiarism' includes, but is not limited to, the use, by paraphrase or direct quotation, of the published or unpublished work of another person without full and clear acknowledgment. It also includes the unacknowledged use of materials prepared by another person or agency engaged in the selling of term papers or other academic materials."

We should add here that plagiarism isn't just a concern at WSU. Established scholars, politicians, and journalists, among others, have all suffered professionally because they passed off the work of someone else as if it was their own.

©Jurgenfr/Shutterstock.com

Plagiarism is easy to commit and also easy to detect.

Sometimes plagiarism is so obvious that it would be laughable if the issue wasn't so serious. In fall 2015 one of us was presented with a paper on the history of the Barbie doll (a strange but valid topic, and one that shows the diversity of interests of WSU students). It just didn't look right so we did a little research. All of the text was plagiarized from a source that was not acknowledged. And two cited sources did not appear to exist.

Today's college students quite literally are awash in information (but don't assume that high *quantity* equals high *quality*). With so many resources available on the Web it is easy, and maybe tempting, to just cut-and-paste text into a paper you are writing. This is plagiarism, of course, and you will be caught. Some students fail to see that the font used in their stolen text is different from that in the rest of their paper. Or that the style of writing may be totally different in one paragraph compared to others. It has never been easier to catch cut-and-paste plagiarists. Like you, we can use Google. We can type in a chunk of text from your paper to see if there's a match. Or, we can check your text with SafeAssign, an anti-plagiarism tool that is part of the Blackboard learning management system used by WSU. There are also other software packages out there, such as Turnitin, that will compare the papers you write to hundreds if not thousands of samples in a database.

Actually, Turnitin handily identifies the most common kinds of plagiarism. You must avoid all of them like the plague:

- *Cloning*, or passing off someone else's work as your own, word for word.
- *Mashup*, or mixing material copied from multiple sources.
- *CTRL-C* (control-copy on your keyboard), or taking big chunks of text from a single source without alteration.

Plagiarism is slippery because you can do it without realizing it (unlike our very deliberate friends with wandering eyes and inky hands, or the Barbie historian). Let's say you are writing a paper in a class on Latin American literature and you want to include some text from a novel written by Colombian author Gabriel Garcia Marquez (he won the Nobel Prize for Literature in 1982). You should put his text in quotation marks and provide an acknowledgment:

> "'She was lost in her longing to understand.' (*Love in the Time of Cholera*, Gabriel Garcia Marquez, 1985)."

But you don't. Perhaps you didn't know the appropriate format. Or maybe you were in such a hurry that you simply forgot. In both of these instances you weren't deliberately trying to fool us by plagiarizing, but your motivation doesn't matter. You plagiarized and we must respond appropriately, with serious repercussions for you.

Try this test. Read the following few sentences from an important article on multitasking written by Annie Paul and published online in the magazine *Slate* on May 3 2013 (note that we just acknowledged who wrote this piece of writing, and where and when it was published):

> "But evidence from psychology, cognitive science, and neuroscience suggests that when students multitask while doing schoolwork, their learning is far spottier and shallower than if the work had their full attention. They understand and remember less, and they have greater difficulty transferring their learning to new contexts."

Here are two versions of this important piece of text, both written by us. Which one is an example of plagiarism?

> Version One. "As Annie Paul reports in *Slate* (5-3-2013), multitasking results in incomplete and superficial learning, according to research done by scientists who study human brains and behavior. Students remember less of their schoolwork, and what they do remember is harder for them to comprehend and use in novel ways."

Version Two. "Evidence from work done by psychologists, cognitive scientists, and neuro-scientists suggests that multitasking by students while doing schoolwork results in spotty and shallow learning. Students understand and remember less, and it is more difficult for them to transfer what they have learned to new contexts."

While neither version is identical to the words written by Annie Paul, Version Two is far more similar in both the words used and their ordering. Also, there's no attribution of this piece of text to its author, or where and when it was published. We consider Version Two to be an example of plagiarism.

If all of this sounds fierce, it is because scholars don't cheat. It is your responsibility to be aware of policies related to academic integrity. Read your syllabi, talk to your advisor and instructors, and maybe visit the Undergraduate Writing Center (in the Smith Center for Undergraduate Education, room 303).

WORKSHEET 9
READ: SCHOLARS DON'T CHEAT—ACADEMIC INTEGRITY

Plagiarism comes in two forms: intentional and unintentional. An obvious example (we hope) of intentional plagiarism is when you copy an essay from a friend or a chunk of text from Wikipedia. However, unintentional plagiarism is often not so obvious and it is imperative that you are aware of it. Hopefully, this worksheet exercise will help.

Read the following paragraph and the two versions that follow. For each version, decide if it constitutes plagiarism, then underline the parts that indicate plagiarism and change them so that there is no plagiarism.

ORIGINAL PARAGRAPH

"Today's college students quite literally are awash in information. With so many resources available on the Web it is easy, and maybe tempting, to just cut-and-paste text into a paper you are writing. This is plagiarism, of course, and you will be caught. Some students fail to see that the font used in their stolen text is different from that in the rest of their paper. Or the style of writing may be totally different in one paragraph compared to others. It has never been easier to catch cut-and-paste plagiarists. Like you, we can use Google. We can type in a chunk of text from your paper and see if there's a match. There are also some commercial software systems, such as Turnitin, that will compare your paper to hundreds if not thousands of samples in a database" (Verrell and McCabe, 2016).

VERSION NUMBER ONE, WRITTEN BY ROCKY

Today's students are literally awash in knowledge. With multiple resources available on the Internet it is easy to just cut-and-paste text into a paper you are writing and submit it as your own. This is copying or cheating and this is not allowed. Some students, in their haste, don't even recognize that their font is different from that used in the stolen text. Or the style of writing may be totally different in one paragraph compared to others. It used to be difficult to catch plagiarists. However, now it is very easy, and we can type in a chunk of text from your paper and see if there's a match.

VERSION NUMBER TWO, WRITTEN BY CHLOE

Today's students are steeped in enormous quantities of information, and the number of sources is mindboggling. With many resources available on the Internet, and content which is exactly what you wanted to say, it is easy to just cut-and-paste text into a paper you are writing and submit it as your own (Verrell and McCabe, 2016). This may be plagiarism and you are responsible for knowing the difference between word-for-word paraphrasing, which constitutes plagiarism, and legitimate paraphrasing, which is not plagiarism. Some students, in their haste, don't even recognize that their font is different from that used in the stolen text. Or the style of writing may be totally different in one paragraph compared to others. It used to be difficult to catch plagiarists. However, now it is very easy, and we can type in a chunk of text from your paper and see if there's a match.

NOW REWRITE CHLOE'S VERSION WITHOUT PLAGIARISM

Please make and attach a copy of Timetable One from Worksheet One and modify or edit it to reflect your actual timetable during the last week (be honest).

CHAPTER 10
LIVING ON AND WORKING IN A DIVERSE AND INCLUSIVE CAMPUS

More people in the U.S. are going on to higher education now than ever before. And as the college population is growing bigger it is also growing more diverse. We wrote this book to provide suggestions for becoming a scholar that are relevant to *all* WSU students. In this chapter we consider students from specific backgrounds who may have particular educational, social or other needs. WSU's goal is to create an inclusive atmosphere and to ensure the academic success of all students. No student will be left behind in these respects. Therefore, meeting the specific needs of students who identify with certain groups shall not isolate them from others—we must aim for inclusivity and encourage interaction. WSU offers a plethora of programs and services to students who identify as multicultural, LGBTQ+, and First-Generation, as well as programs specific to students with disabilities, women students, international students, transfer, and non-traditional students. We are very grateful to our colleague Courtney Benjamin for her help in bringing many of these to our attention.

MULTICULTURAL STUDENTS

Across the US, students of color are the fastest-growing segment of the university student body. This includes students who identify as African-American, Asian or Pacific Islander, Chicano/Latino, and Native American. About 35% of first-year students admitted to WSU in the fall of 2017 identified as belonging to a non-white population. Historically, there have been many barriers to success for these students and very sadly, too many remain in place today, especially for those who fall into the absurdly surreal category of being "illegal people." WSU recognizes the importance of offering services and supports to enhance the educational quality and experience of all students of color. There are many great programs offered by the Office of Multicultural Student Services (www .mss.wsu.edu), including a student mentoring program and individual advising services.

LGBTQ+

Social scientists have long recognized the complexity and diversity of human sexuality and gender identity, and (finally) society is catching up. A recent poll found that just over half of Americans surveyed support same-sex marriage. And as we write these words, the civil rights of transgender people are being discussed as never before (real change begins but doesn't end with discussion). For WSU students who identify as LGBTQ+, and for anyone who wishes to learn more and be a supportive ally, providing a safe and welcoming environment is the function of the Gender Identity/ Expression and Sexual Orientation Resource Center: www.thecenter.wsu.edu

FIRST IN THE FAMILY

About 40% of undergraduates at WSU are the first members of their families to take their education beyond high school. Lovingly referred to as "First-Gen" students, it can be hard to navigate along all of the twists and turns that a college career entails. And sometimes, it might feel that you're navigating this road alone without a family-based understanding of what college life is all about. But you don't have to be alone because WSU has many resources to help. Two of these programs include the First Scholars Program (www. firstscholars.wsu.edu) and the College Assistance for Migrants Program, or CAMP (http://camp.wsu. edu). Check them out, because these programs can really boost the odds that first-year First-Gen students stay to become sophomore First-Gen students.

STUDENTS WITH DISABILITIES

Paraphrasing from WSU's website (and so avoiding plagiarism), the University makes available accommodations and resources of all sorts to students with disabilities, psychological or physical illnesses, or temporary injuries that could restrict their access to the kinds of educational opportunities enjoyed by their peers. And so a deaf student may have an aide who translates an instructor's spoken words into American Sign Language (ASL). Or a student with attention-deficit/hyperactivity disorder (ADHD) may be provided with a quiet place in which to take exams.

Examples of services available include testing accommodations (a place with few distractions, extended time, etc), note-taking, alternative print media, and training in time management and organizational skills. Students who wish to be considered for such assistance should contact the Access Center at www.accesscenter.wsu.edu.

WOMEN STUDENTS

As with all of the groups of students we have included in this chapter, the needs of women students are largely those of all WSU undergraduates. Regardless of ethnicity and sexual orientation, students who identify as female do have some specific resources available to them. These include health-related services, a place for child and family amenities (including a safe and quiet place to pump breast milk if the student is also a new mother), and information and services to protect against harassment and assault (and support if they occur). They also provide places to meet new friends and get involved in issues concerning women. Check out the Women's Center as a starting point: www.women.wsu.edu

FROM DISTANT SHORES

International students come to WSU from other countries to study for a bachelor's or graduate degree. Students from nearly 100 foreign countries are studying at WSU as we write this in the spring of 2018. International students for whom English is not a first language must take a test to demonstrate linguistic competence, but our experience is that language barriers can nevertheless be substantial. In addition, international students are isolated from family and friends, and may find themselves in a culture and educational system that is very unfamiliar. Often international students seek out and socialize with others from their own country, and while this offers a robust support system, it can be isolating and slow the further development of English language and American social skills. Then there's the rather daunting task of making sure that federal immigration regulations are followed. This includes obtaining an appropriate visa, and abiding by the conditions of the visa with regard to course enrollment and required GPA. These challenges need not be overwhelming, and we encourage international students to make full use of all of the resources available at WSU, especially those offered by the Office of International Programs. Go to www.ip.wsu.edu. In addition, everyone is invited to the International Center in the CUB to learn more about global diversity of cultures and traditions.

OLDER (AND WISER?)

Our emphasis has been on the transition that students make as they move from high school to college, and then beyond. But 'typical' first-year students (late teens, right out of high school) are in a majority that is slowly shrinking. A recent analysis predicts that, between 2011 and 2021, there will be a 14% increase in the enrollment in college of students who are at least 25 years of age. A somewhat extreme example of a "mature" student is Betty Reilly of Florida, who recently earned her B.A. in English at 89 years of age.

So-called nontraditional students are already with us, and they're a growing and diverse population, including older people who:

- Didn't graduate from high school, but who later earned a GED.
- Left high school and went into the Armed Services.
- Left and went straight into the workforce.
- Transfer to four-year institutions like WSU from two-year colleges.
- Are employed at the same time as they are enrolled in college part-time.

Such students may be looking to satisfy curiosity, obtain necessary training for employment or develop a pre-existing career. But while much of what we've written so far is relevant to all undergraduates, including nontraditional ones, some of the challenges faced by people attending college later in life can generate both excitement and anxiety.

First, we suggest that you consider taking things a little slowly (see also Chapter Seven). Study habits might be a bit rusty, and it can take a while to resharpen them. In addition, some nontraditional students need to juggle their studies with family responsibilities and jobs—a recent study found that about two of every three adult, working students experience significant anxiety. Taking things slowly, most obviously by not taking too many classes in early semesters, allows for an adjustment by students and, in some cases, their family members. As we've said before, the winner in higher education isn't the person who finishes *first*, it's the person who finishes *best*. That said, you do want enough early momentum to keep you moving forward.

We don't have data, but experience leads us to suspect that first-year students too often attend college with unclear goals in mind, at least at first. In addition, too often is the bill for college picked-up by someone else (maybe the "Bank of Mom and Dad") or by financial aid (which might not always be understood as a loan that has to be repaid). In our experience, many nontraditional students have a clearer goal in sight, and are more aware of the costs of college even if someone else is paying (as might be true for a veteran under the G.I. Bill).

©Wavebreakmedia/Shutterstock.com

Nontraditional students are a rapidly growing segment of higher education in the United States.

Our second recommendation is to have a plan. Everyone needs a plan, of course—and everyone needs at least a Plan B (if not C and D, too) to go with Plan A. But a clear view of the directions needed to attain goals can be of particular significance to nontraditional students, who often have more responsibilities and a keener sense of the passing of time than their younger classmates. Your academic advisor can help you explore the resources that WSU has to help you develop a clear pathway to graduation . . . and beyond.

Third, nontraditional students sometimes tell us they feel a bit isolated. Even though their numbers are growing, some feel swamped by their younger peers. While most mature students are not what are affectionately known as "geezers" or "old fogies," they still might find members of the Millennial Generation to be not quite like themselves in terms of interests and maturity. We aren't aware of any clubs or other organizations that specifically cater to nontraditional students at WSU. There seems to be a vacant niche to be filled, perhaps by you but not in your first semester.

Fourth, a quick word on transferring academic credits to WSU. Students with such transfers are largely of three kinds:

- They took Running Start courses at a community college while in high school (if Washington residents).
- They took Advanced Placement courses while in high school.
- They graduated from high school and took courses at a community college, perhaps going as far as earning an associate degree (in Arts, Science or Applied Science).

For all three kinds of students (plus a smaller number who come with International Baccalaureate credits or transfer credits from other four-year colleges), some of whom may be nontraditional, the academic credits they earned elsewhere may transfer to WSU, taking the place of courses that they might or would take at WSU. Note that we write "may transfer" because you should not take transfer of such credits for granted. We can't go into all of the details regarding the transfer of credits here, but a good place to start searching for information is the WSU Transfer Clearinghouse (www.transfercredit.wsu.edu). In addition, an academic advisor can help you to make sure that appropriate credits earned elsewhere are incorporated into your WSU program of study.

WORKSHEET 10

READ: LIVING ON AND WORKING IN A DIVERSE AND INCLUSIVE CAMPUS

"Diversity" has become a bit of a buzzword in recent years. It has also become a political tool, sometimes used for good but not always. There's no question that, while all members of our human family share a huge amount in common, we aren't all the same. We differ from others in terms of wealth, religious belief, and sexual orientation, to name a few. Some differences may lie in our biology, others in our family histories and life experiences.

Part of a college education is to learn about and appreciate diversity, and to develop an understanding of and respect for people who are different from us, both within the United States and beyond. This is the learning outcome of the Diversity, or DIVR, classes that are included in University Core Requirements (UCORE). Your greatest learning experience in this regard will come from living and working day-to-day with people who aren't the same as you.

Each one of us can be a teacher and a learner at the same time, but let's acknowledge that this might not be easy. Some parts of this reflective exercise might not be easy.

1. We all have certain biases: what are some of yours? Can you change your biases or are they fixed? Are all biases negative?

2. The words "diversity" and "inclusiveness" are used a lot these days, but they aren't always defined. What do they mean to you?

3. Recall a situation in which you were different in some noticeable way from everyone else around you. Write a paragraph to address the following questions. How were you different and how did it feel? How were you treated by others? How would you have liked to be treated by others? What might be some benefits of being different from most of the people around you?

4. We achieve our goals through hard work. But isn't there also an element of luck or good fortune in what we achieve and own? In what ways are you lucky? Were their specific aspects of your upbringing that influenced how you were lucky? How might you level the playing field to help those less fortunate than yourself?

5. Most of us have some feature about ourselves that might separate us from others and which might put us in the position of needing additional assistance and support. Think about your own needs, and then visit some of the websites mentioned in Chapter 10. After visiting these sites, write a few paragraphs on what you would find useful and helpful in your own journey toward graduation.

> **Please make and attach a copy of Timetable One from Worksheet One and modify or edit it to reflect your actual timetable during the last week (be honest).**

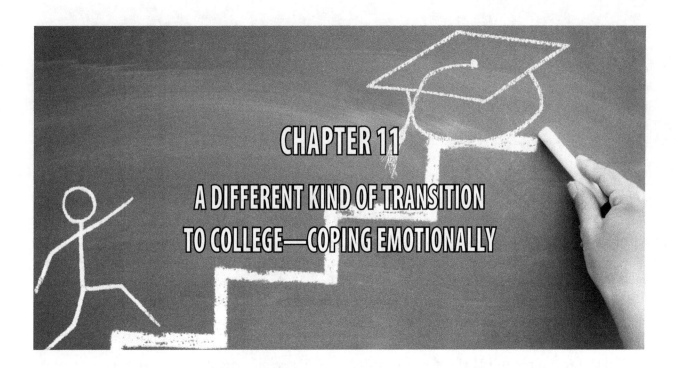

CHAPTER 11
A DIFFERENT KIND OF TRANSITION TO COLLEGE—COPING EMOTIONALLY

Most discussions of college readiness focus on competency in terms of basic math and language skills. Fewer address study skills and habits of mind, the focus of much of this book. And even fewer explore what we'll call here "emotional readiness." We consider this to be an extremely important issue that often receives too little attention. Indeed, a national survey published in 2017 reported that 60% of students wish they'd received more help in preparing emotionally for college. If you also feel like that, know that you aren't alone. And know that, in time, that feeling will pass.

You should expect your first semester at WSU at least, if not your first year and a bit beyond, to be challenging emotionally. Almost everyone will feel like this, although those feelings will diminish and vanish over time for most people. You're in an unfamiliar place, separated from family and old friends. Of course, what's novel now will become familiar as time goes on. You'll surely make new friends, perhaps best friends forever, but some relationships won't go so well. Add to that the fact that you are taking on responsibilities that may be novel and even uncomfortable. As we discussed earlier, you're in charge of managing your time and your money in ways that may well be unfamiliar. You might fall prey to the temptation of bad habits, such as binge drinking. And now add further the fact that you are one of 20,000 or so students in Pullman, and perhaps one of as many as 500 or so in a single class. You might feel a bit lonely. Perhaps when checking your grade on your first college exam you find that you earned a C or a D, or even an F—for the first time ever (many of us feel that too great an emphasis is placed on A grades in high school). While we must stress that you should welcome difficulty, that it's OK to fail (not all the time, of course), and that you can learn by making mistakes, we also understand that unexpectedly poor grades can be a big source of stress. Perhaps getting a tutor might help your performance: check out www.tutoring.ascc.wsu.edu. (We like this quote from President Teddy Roosevelt: "It is hard to fail, but it is worse never to have tried to succeed.")

You need to know that feelings of loneliness and disappointment are *totally* natural and to be expected, especially early on. Think about it—your life got turned upside down. Know that those feelings are completely normal, and that they'll almost certainly fade away as time goes on. New opportunities and the new friends that they bring will help you to establish a new balance in your life, what some call a "new norm." The same will be true as you learn to navigate the academic aspects of college.

KEEP IN TOUCH

For many, but not only, first-year students, college is a mix of eager anticipation and uncertain expectation. But even as you make new friends you don't have to abandon old ones—old friends and family aren't as far away as they might seem, thanks to the easy availability of social media.

The last thing you need is for your parents to be hovering over your every move, so-called "helicopter parents." But as parents ourselves, let us ask that you not forget Mom and Dad. Even if you don't miss them too much, they'll certainly miss you—after all, they've had you for 18 years or so. Even "old people" like parents can master such media as FaceTime, Snapchat, and texting (not to mention the phone). Drop Mom and Dad a line every so often: "Hi guys, all is well here. Weather OK, making friends, and getting decent grades. Miss you both."

Let's add a few more words about helicopter parents. These are parents who have been intricately involved with many, maybe all, aspects of your decision-making up to this point. Some would say that helicopter parenting has led to a generation of people who are unable to make decisions. Some would also say that helicopter parenting has led to a generation of people that is unable to show empathy, because parents have not allowed their children to fail, or experience feelings of sadness or disappointment. These are huge subjects that we are sure you are aware of, and it would be beneficial to reflect on your ability, and the ability of your friends, to make decisions (significant or not) that will affect your college success. Have you thought about empathy? Is it important to you, and how will it affect your college experience? If you or your friends are feeling overwhelmed (see next section), will you be able to support each other?

"IT'S ALL TOO MUCH!"

It is easy to feel overwhelmed emotionally. National data on the psychological problems experienced by college students, many stemming from the kinds of emotional issues mentioned above, are rather sobering. We also have 2017 numbers specifically for WSU, which show that, in a 12-month period:

- 47% of students sometimes felt that their situations were hopeless.
- 36% sometimes were too depressed to function properly.
- 25% were diagnosed with (but not necessarily treated for) depression or an anxiety disorder (such as panic attacks).
- 9% had thoughts about suicide.

These are scary numbers, but we share them with you to inform rather than frighten. It is important that you know that emotional stress happens but is not inevitable. It is also important for you to know that WSU has resources to help, and that asking for help is a sign of strength, not weakness. Counseling and Psychological Services (www.counsel.wsu.edu) and Health and Wellness Services

©Creativa Images/Shutterstock.com

Sometimes it might feel overwhelming, but help is out there. Check out the resources available and bookmark them now in case you need them in the future.

(www.hws.wsu.edu) provide workshops on mental health issues, and have trained professionals waiting to help you cope with and overcome emotional stress. We can't encourage you strongly enough to take advantage of all they offer. In fact, WSU has developed what is called the AWARE Network to provide even more support (www.aware.wsu.edu). It includes the programs mentioned above as well as the Dean of Students (www.deanofstudents.wsu.edu) and WSU Police (www.police.wsu.edu). Students who feel they need help can contact the AWARE Network, as can students who think that their friends may benefit from the help that is offered.

Another resource, mentioned earlier, is the Access Center (www.accesscenter.wsu.edu), which works with instructors to make accommodations for people with psychological as well as physical disabilities, such as depression and deafness. For example, a student who is documented to have a condition affecting his or her memory may be given additional time to complete exams. Unfortunately, we live in a society where there is still a lot of stigma associated with cognitive and mental health issues. Know that you are not alone and that you will not be judged—help is at hand. And appreciate that, nationally, about 20% of our U.S. population live with some kind of mental health condition every year. It isn't a sign of immaturity or weakness to ask for help if you think you might need it. Rather, it is a sign of maturity and considerable courage.

We came across what we think is a very useful way of thinking about your mental health, developed by Dr Gregg Henriques, a psychologist at James Madison University in Virginia. He suggests that you develop an "inner eye" that monitors how you think about the stresses that are part of college life (and beyond). Dr Henriques encourages you to look at yourself with an inner eye that is CALM. Here's our interpretation of what he means:

- C = curious: ask why you are feeling as you do. Can you find a reason?
- A = accepting: don't judge yourself too harshly—appreciate that it's only human to feel down sometimes.
- L = loving: show yourself some compassion. Appreciate that, even if things aren't going so well right now, you are still a person of value, someone who matters.
- M = motivated: don't lose sight of the things you are passionate about, things that give you enjoyment and your life meaning.

Following the "Keep Calm" meme that seems to be everywhere these days, we agree with Dr Henriques—keep CALM and look within. And yet, even with a CALM inner eye, someone suffering from depression may actually fail to recognize they have a problem or realize its seriousness. You can help by keeping an "outer eye" on your fellow students, watching out for signs of depression so that you can lend a helping hand. These signs include:

- Lack of pleasure in things that were pleasurable before.
- Preferring to spend time alone.
- Pushing other people away.
- Changes in body weight.
- Changes in sleep patterns, especially insomnia.

In addition, there are things you can do for yourself to help ease the stress of college life. In a recent national survey, students listed the following stress relievers:

- Hanging out with friends—100% said they do this when feeling stressed.
- Watching a movie—80% (of course, you can do this with friends).
- Exercise—55% (perhaps with friends—more on this later).

Note that all of the above activities either do or can involve other people. We belong to a very social species, and flesh-and-blood interactions with other people run deeply back into our evolutionary history. There's no doubt to us that too many people choose to interact with others electronically rather than in person, and that this can only compound the problem of loneliness. Psychologist Jean Twenge, at San Diego State University, has found that smartphone use may be directly responsible for depression and feelings of alienation in younger people (and a national survey reports that about 60% of us sleep with our phones right next to our beds!). Most of your Facebook "friends" really aren't friends at all.

©Ross Petukhov/Shutterstock.com

> *Physical exercise is good for your mind and your mood, as well as your muscles.*

MINDFUL MEDITATION

If you are like us, your mind seems like it's always racing, too often reliving the past and worrying about the future: "Why didn't I get an oil change last week?" "What if they close Snoqualmie Pass at the weekend?". We'd like to encourage you to take a time-out by developing what we'll call mindful meditation.

This practice is rooted in a number of eastern traditions, especially Buddhism. It involves letting go of everything—thoughts, feelings, and sensations—except for the present. There's a huge self-help literature on mindfulness that you might like to explore (Google it), but here's a CliffsNotes version of a technique known as attention-based breath meditation (there are other kinds, as you'll find on Google). Sit quietly and gradually focus your attention on breathing. Feel how your abdomen and chest move as you inhale and exhale, and how it feels as the air moves in and out of your nostrils. Try to focus only on those sensations. If your mind starts to wander ("What's for dinner?" "I must start writing that paper."), accept those thoughts and then let them drift away as you refocus on breathing in the moment. Meditate like this for as long as you can maintain your focus, gradually doing so for a little longer each time.

Give it a try—we have, and we'll admit it isn't easy. But there's scientific evidence that mindful meditation can reduce feelings of stress, anxiety, and depression, and even physical pain. And for what it's worth, mindful meditation has been endorsed by the U.S. military and the NBA.

GET A PET

The biologist Edward Wilson, now retired from Harvard, has suggested that the affection and connection that humans feel to the living world is actually something that evolved in our distant ancestors. Whether or not that's true, there is growing evidence that interacting with plants and non-human animals can relieve stress and anxiety. Get a plant or two for your room-one study found that interacting with houseplants can improve mood and even lower blood pressure. Think about getting a pet, making sure you follow WSU's housing regulations. Even caring for an insect can improve psychological well-being, as shown in a Japanese study in which people kept caged crickets as pets! And if you don't want an animal of your own, borrow someone else's. Interacting with a therapy dog before exams can reduce your stress level for several hours afterward (so can writing a brief essay on the things that most stress you out).

PUSHING BEYOND YOUR COMFORT ZONE

There's a bit more. Every person who goes to college brings with him or her certain beliefs, opinions, and dogmas to which he or she may adhere very closely. One goal of higher education is to present you with new and different ways of seeing the world and your place in it, and this might challenge some core values that you hold. For example, a biology class on evolution might challenge your literal belief in the Biblical account of Creation. Or a class on gender studies might challenge your belief that homosexuality is a wicked life-style choice. Be aware that, although challenges to your own point of view might be uncomfortable, such challenges are precisely what it takes for you to grow intellectually. You should welcome them rather than dread or reject them. And of course, understanding and respecting diverse views is necessary if you are to be a responsible citizen.

There's a big and rather fierce debate going on at the moment about whether instructors should provide students with so-called "trigger warnings." These essentially alert students that some of the material in a class may cause them psychological distress, and so enable sensitive students to avoid that material or seek alternative means of coping. Every person who goes to college has a history. For example, one person may once have been assaulted sexually. Another may have served in Iraq or Afghanistan. Both of these people may suffer from post-traumatic stress disorder (PTSD), where triggering memories of aggression may result in considerable distress. Such triggers could arise in a class on, say, how the media portray conflict and violence.

Be aware that, although some instructors at WSU may provide trigger warnings, others do not—there's no University requirement that they be provided. All we wish to stress here is that the contents of college classes can be distressing for some students as well as challenging (hopefully) for all. If after reading a syllabus you suspect that some of the content of that class may cause you distress, talk to your instructor about your options.

KEEP YOUR EYES ON THE PRIZE: GET GRITTY

There's one more emotional issue we need to mention, and that's the importance of being able to cope with disappointment. For some of you, earning good grades in high school might not have involved too much effort. In college, grades can be disappointing even though you try hard.

Let's be 100% frank—you will trip and stumble in college, such as when you earn that first C or D grade (easily said, we know, but don't panic and treat it as an incentive to do better next time). Coping with the disappointments you will experience might be difficult. One of the big buzzwords you'll hear these days perhaps rather overused, is "grit.", coined by psychologist Angela Duckworth of the University of Pennsylvania. As an example, we talk about athletes having grit when they show purpose, passion, and perseverance (in addition to raw talent: try as hard as we might, even with Carol Dweck's growth mindsets, neither of we authors will ever be elite athletes). We want you to show grit as a college student. Set yourself a goal (your purpose), understanding that, in the shorter term, a broad goal is often more attainable than a narrower one (for example, you are more likely to reach the dieting goal of losing about 10 lbs than reaching your ideal weight of 185.57 lbs). Develop and maintain the motivation to reach that goal (your passion). Should you trip and stumble—say, flunk a class—don't just quit. Dust yourself off and keep moving forward (your perseverance, sometimes called resilience). That doesn't mean that you shouldn't evaluate whether your goal is really the right one for you. There's no value to hitting your head against a brick wall, of course, but if you feel like quitting then remind yourself of why you are here and what you want to achieve. As we said, don't just quit. Follow the three Ps: purpose, passion, and perseverance.

And let us stress, yet again, that while *you* are ultimately responsible for your success in college, there's a whole team behind you that's ready to help. We've already mentioned www.conduct.wsu. edu/resources as a wonderful site to explore WSU- and community-based resources that provide assistance to students. Just remember that asking for help when you need it isn't a sign of immaturity or weakness—it is a sign of maturity and strength.

WORKSHEET 11

READ: A DIFFERENT KIND OF TRANSITION TO COLLEGE—COPING EMOTIONALLY

The bottom line is that if you are *only* having fun in college, then there's something very wrong (unless you are a genius). College is meant to be challenging academically. Sure, some of your classes will be easy but certainly not all. You will have to cope with exams and papers and deadlines. You might get sick, you might party a little too hearty, and a relationship or two might "go south." Inevitably you will get stressed, maybe *very* stressed. A little stress is apparently a good thing because, with the help of adrenaline, it heightens our awareness and sharpens our reactions. After all, we wouldn't be here if our ancestors hadn't been able to outsmart saber-toothed tigers! However too much stress can be bad for your health and hurt your ability to be a successful scholar and to earn a degree.

1. You need to recognize when you are stressed. List three signs that indicate you are stressed.

    a.

    b.

    c.

2. You need to recognize things that trigger stress in you. List three triggers.

    a.

    b.

    c.

3. You need to know where you can get help, and to get help sooner rather than later. List three resources on campus that can help if you need it. For each resource, give the help that it provides.

   a.

   b.

   c.

Please make and attach a copy of Timetable One from Worksheet One and modify or edit it to reflect your actual timetable during the last week (be honest).

While our focus in this book has been on the life of the mind, we must say just a little about looking after your body while in college. That physical exercise has both bodily and mental benefits has been known for a while. For example, a study of students at Purdue University in Indiana found that students' GPAs increased with increase in the number of times they went to the gym. In addition, exercise, especially if aerobic (such as filling your lungs by running or dancing), can help a person deal with the anxiety and depression that can come with the stress of being in a new place with new people doing new things (which sounds a bit like going to college). Clearly you can care for your body and your mind at the same time. WSU has an amazing Rec Center as well as many opportunities to engage in intramural sports. We encourage you to enjoy all that's available, but just make sure that fitting such recreational activities into your schedule doesn't displace academic ones.

TOO MANY CALORIES

You may have heard of the "Freshman 15," which refers to the amount of weight, in pounds, that students are said to gain in their first year of college—actually, weight gain is more like 5-10-ish lbs from first to final year. All-you-can-eat pizza sounds great, but too much pepperoni can easily lead to too many pounds. Fruits and veggies are available in WSU's dining facilities, and mixing them into your diet makes obvious sense. And for those of you who choose to drink alcohol, knowing that doing so is against the law if you are under 21 years of age or on WSU property, do remember that liquor is full of empty calories that can easily pack on the pounds.

TOO LITTLE SLEEP

It isn't unusual for students to answer "I'm so tired" if we ask "How are you doing?" People in their late teens, the typical age of first-year college students, need around 7-9-ish hours of sleep per night (some authorities say more). The actual average time spent sleeping is closer to a little over 7 hours.

In addition to sleeping perhaps too little overall, college students typically show too little consistency in their sleep habits, skipping hours on some occasions, and oversleeping on others. You need enough sleep and you need it in the right pattern.

We cannot stress enough the importance of proper sleep to both physical and mental health. In terms of the former, poor sleep habits are associated with weight gain in some people, largely because of increased food intake. In terms of mental health, poor sleep habits may be associated with depression. If good academic performance relies on a healthy brain and mind, which it surely does, then evidence shows that poor sleep habits are a good predictor of withdrawal from, and dropping of, classes by first-year college students. In fact, one study found that poor sleep predicted lowered academic performance better than did alcohol and marijuana use. To learn more about good sleeping habits, check out the "Sleep More, Sleep Better" program offered by WSU's Health and Wellness folks.

We suggest you walk or bike the hills of Pullman, even the steep ones. Forget the car or bus. There's evidence to suggest that physical exercise, especially aerobic exercise like brisk walking, strengthens the connections between nerve cells in the brain, and can slow cognitive decline in older adults. And so eat well, sleep well, and exercise well—both your body and your brain will thank you for it, now and in the future.

"It's always nice to see my students
jumping with energy first thing in the morning."

CHAPTER 13

THE SOCIAL STUDENT

College isn't just a place to grow intellectually, although we think that is its primary purpose, as you should too. It is also a place where you should grow as a person, a place to mature and develop further your sense of who you are and how you fit in with all around you, including your peers. Indeed, many students regard college as the best time of their life, often we suspect more because of social rather than academic aspects.

SOCIAL BUT SILLY

Here's good news. In 2017, an organization known as the National Council for Home Safety and Security ranked Pullman as the 5th safest city in Washington, and WSU as the 5th safest college in the nation. But 100% safety just isn't possible. We have to deal with the serious stuff upfront. You're away from home, perhaps for the first time. The temptations you face are many, but perhaps the biggest is the use and perhaps abuse of alcohol. You know that you cannot legally consume alcoholic beverages until you are 21 years of age, and even then not in public or on WSU property. But let's be honest, it isn't too hard for younger college students to get access to liquor of some kind. National statistics suggest that as many as eight out of every 10 college students drink alcohol, and that about four out of those eight drinkers are binge drinkers. By one definition, a binge drinker consumes four or five alcoholic drinks in a two-hour period on at least one day per month.

We aren't just talking here about minor-in-possession (MIP) offenses. Alcohol (and other substances too, such as marijuana) is involved in other crimes in Pullman, including driving under the influence (DUI), sexual assault, domestic violence, and burglary. In some burglary cases, students get so drunk that they enter residences other than their own, more through mistake than malice. More serious are instances when intoxicated students fall out of windows or from roofs—yes, these happen. In one very sad case a few years ago, a drunk student from the nearby University of Idaho died from hypothermia, probably because he was unable to find his way home. It really is scary that national statistics indicate that around 2,000 students die each year from unintended harm inflicted by alcohol consumption.

We need here to say a word or two about safety on WSU's campus. Home burglary and motor theft came close to the top of a recent survey of threats to campus safety, stressing that you need to keep your property secure. Then there's the difficult subject of sexual assault. Even though WSU is a pretty safe campus, sexual assaults do occur here as they do at colleges and universities across the nation. National statistics suggest that one in every four or five college women may be assaulted sexually, and one in about every 16 men (many assaults occur during the so-called Red Zone, between the start of the school year and Thanksgiving). Do bear in mind that assault rates don't always include harassment without physical assault, and that actual rapes are not always reported. In October 2017, our very own student newspaper, *The Daily Evergreen*, reported 15 sexual assaults in Pullman. Any number of published assaults above zero is intolerable, and do please remember that not all assaults are reported to the authorities. WSU has no tolerance for such behavior, and no one, woman or man, should feel unsafe on any of our campuses. We all need to work to banish sexual assault from WSU, and education of both sexes is paramount. You can do some pretty simple and yet effective things. Don't drink too much (or even any) alcohol. Pour and then guard your own drinks at parties, and look out to protect your friends' drinks from unwanted additives. Take the buddy-system a step further, and watch who your friends spend time with so you can help them to avoid unwise choices. You can explore this idea of being a buddy through WSU's Green Dot program: www.hws.wsu.edu/green-dot. Be prepared to intervene boldly but safely yourself, and always remember that calling 911 is the best option if you're in even one ounce of doubt.

For women leaving campus after a late lab or discussion session, there was until October of 2016 a great service that provided door-to-door rides. Known as Women's Transit, this service has been replaced by Cougar Safe Rides, which operates between 10 PM and 2 AM Thursday through Saturday. Just call or text WSU-267-SAFE. There's also the Cougar Security Escort Program, providing a partner to walk with you on campus—call (509) 335-8548. And there are Emergency Blue Phones dotted around the campus for anyone who feels uncomfortable as they go from place to place. Pick up a phone if things don't feel right and you'll be put through to the police department. Let's not be neurotic but let's certainly be careful.

©View Apart/Shutterstock.com

Alcohol is not just unhealthy if consumed excessively, but drinking it is also illegal for most WSU students. Why risk your future with an MIP conviction? It could jeopardize you getting an apartment, a job, and more.

Nationally, about one in every four college students has abused some kind of drug, and marijuana is probably the drug that is most readily available (national data indicate increasing campus use of marijuana, with decreasing use for some other drugs). Although the recreational consumption of marijuana is now legal in Washington, this is *not* the case for individuals, even if aged 21 years of age or older, who are on WSU property (this has more to do with federal restrictions on marijuana use than state ones, although the distinction doesn't really matter—just *don't do it*).

More national data indicate that about 10% of students misuse prescription stimulants, such as Adderall, in the belief that these powerful psychotropic drugs will aid in studying and boost grades. Stimulants like Adderall are used in the treatment of clinical conditions such as ADHD, but don't be tempted to take some from a friend who is prescribed them for a legitimate reason. While stimulant drugs may help you to stay awake, their side effects may send you to the emergency room with heart palpitations, extreme anxiety, or even a psychotic episode (with delusions and hallucinations).

Many college students think that they are essentially invincible, that they can do what they want when and where they want (perhaps this isn't such a bad attitude if all it does is to inspire you to success in college and career). A few beers or shots, or a quick joint, might not sound like such a big deal. But consider the potential consequences of engaging in illegal behavior. Do you think that an MIP conviction will make you more competitive for winning your dream job at Microsoft or making it into pharmacy school? Appreciate that the consequences of what you do now can reach far forward into the future.

WSU is committed to educating students on the negative consequences of making poor choices in terms of alcohol and drug use, as well as imprudent sexual activity. All students coming to WSU who are under 21 years of age are required to attend a workshop entitled *Booze, Sex, and Reality Checks*, and complete a Web-based survey on alcohol use with personalized feedback (appropriately known as e-Chug: details of these and related programs can be found at www.hws.wsu.edu/bsrc.

And do remember that even if you don't go crazy with "substances," just staying up late can dent your academic performance even if you remain sober. Both of us have seen students in our classes with their heads on their desks, apparently oblivious to the proceedings. A recent national study suggests that lack of sleep may hurt your GPA as much as drinking alcohol and smoking marijuana. It also has been found that the negative effects on academic performance of drinking and smoking are greatest for first-year students. So, alter your behavioral choices accordingly.

SOCIAL AND SENSIBLE

College provides temptations, for sure, but it also provides opportunities for you to be sensibly and safely social. WSU has many dozens of clubs and other organizations that students can join, some more formally recognized than others (the formal ones, known as Registered Student Organizations, number around 300 and can apply for money to fund their activities). A lot of useful information can be found at www.studentinvolvement.wsu.edu. Some clubs are academic (e.g., Zoology Club), some are sporty (e.g., CrossFit Club), and others are multicultural (e.g., the African Friendship Association).

Getting involved in clubs is a great way to meet new people and try new things. It may even be that, over time, you become elected to a leadership position in a club, say as its President or Treasurer. Leadership is a transferable skill appreciated by many employers, and so involvement in a club can be a valuable resume builder as well as an enjoyable experience.

You might be someone who feels that it is important to give back to the community of which you are a part. The Center for Civic Engagement (CCE) (www.cce.wsu.edu) provides opportunities to students to help them grow as people and at the same time provide benefits to their community. The CCE has hundreds of projects in which you can participate, and the diversity of topics covered is huge. You might spend time at a local food bank, or looking after orphaned horses, or helping to build a house, or chatting with folks living in an eldercare facility. And there are a lot more options. There are actually quite a few courses at WSU where community involvement (called service learning) is a requirement that contributes to your final grade. On a slightly selfish note, helping others makes you feel good and it sends a positive message—you are someone who cares about other people. And that's not a bad thing to include in your resume.

©Jdwfoto/Shutterstock.com

Community service, such as building a house with Habitat for Humanity, helps others, makes you feel good, and also sends a positive message to would-be employers. It's a win-win all round, and it's free!

We are strong supporters of students being involved in sensible and safe extracurricular activities; indeed, both of us have served as faculty advisors for Registered Student Organizations. But we suggest you engage in these activities carefully. We have sometimes seen first-year and even older students go rather wild given the opportunities available, with the danger that "*club life*" may eclipse "*class life*." Your job is to find the right balance between the things you have to do and the things you'd like to do, and academics must take priority. And so, our advice is to go slowly on extracurricular activities until you're comfortable that you've succeeded in making the transition to college from high school.

CHAPTER 14

WHY *YOU* BUT NOT *ME*—BEING COMPETITIVE

You live in a competitive age, whether your goal after earning your degree is to go for your dream job or apply to graduate or professional school. It is so very important that you know that in today's marketplace, a good GPA simply isn't enough. As we discussed earlier, acquiring transferable skills, such as (but not only) the ability to communicate effectively, is crucially important, and can be just as important as the major you choose. Ask yourself right now what will make you stand out from the crowd as you move from college to career. Here, we identify some things you should be thinking about now even if you won't need to implement some of them until later.

LETTERS OF RECOMMENDATION

How would you describe yourself to a would-be employer? Diligent? Intelligent? Industrious? Punctual? Friendly? Whether applying for a job, a scholarship, an internship, or a spot in nursing school, you will obviously try as hard as possible to make yourself sound as impressive as possible. And that's why you'll be asked to provide letters of recommendation or reference. These are written by people who, more objectively than yourself, can discuss your qualities and abilities.

All too often, students don't appreciate the importance of such letters in terms of their competitiveness. They especially don't know who to ask for letters. Take a look at this:

"Becky was in my class, earned a B+, and always seemed to be cheerful."

How informative is that? We are often asked to write letters for students we don't know on a personal level, and we really can't write much more than in the example just given.

But imagine that Becky had attended her instructor's office hours (we all have them) and so the instructor got to know more about Becky's interests, motivations, and goals. Now the letter could be more compelling, and might read:

> "Becky earned a B+ in my class, which was close to the top grade in that semester. She was pleasant to talk with, regularly attended office hours, and asked perceptive questions that were linked to both course material and her career goal of training to be a pediatric neurosurgeon."

What kind of letter would you prefer? We appreciate that it might be difficult at first to talk with people you don't know, whether they be professors, teaching assistants, or academic advisors. But it must be done—and most if not all of us are quite pleased to see you when you visit (better to get that letter sooner rather than later, just in case you can't find us down the line). You must make an appointment via e-mail or come to scheduled office hours. The relationship we build won't just be pleasant now—it'll be hugely important a bit later. In fact, a recent survey of college graduates found that the most important and memorable aspects of their college experience were their relationships with peers and professors, and the latter included discussions of diverse ideas and viewpoints outside of class. We don't want to see you only when you have problems, although we do want to stress that asking for help is a sign of strength, not weakness. There's evidence that students perform better if they attend office hours, and some instructors advocate that attendance should be required rather than optional. We believe that the decision of whether you come to see us is your responsibility, one that should be made with encouragement but not coercion. After all, you can only benefit from coming to see us. And you should meet with an academic advisor before you register for classes, whether or not such a meeting is required officially.

HANDS-ON EXPERIENCES

You want to be a vet, but do you know what vets do on a day-to-day basis? You want to be a middle-school teacher, but do you know what kids in that age group are really like? Graduate research sounds great, but do you really know what doing research entails?

We've said it before—it's a competitive world and a good GPA isn't enough. Take our would-be vet. His or her GPA is good, but can the vet school admissions officer be sure that he or she knows what being a vet is really like? The answer is "yes" if he or she completed one or more internships in which he or she worked, perhaps as a volunteer, in a vet clinic or hospital (we have one here at WSU). An internship, paid or not, gives you hands-on experience related to the career in which you are interested. Did our would-be vet perform surgeries on people's pets? Almost certainly not, but he or she did learn a lot about the day-to-day work of a vet, probably mostly shots, spays, and neuters.

The same applies to our would-be teacher. One way he or she could get to know what tweens are like is to volunteer at an after-school program, perhaps coaching baseball or helping with homework.

Then there's our would-be graduate student. Does he or she appreciate how research can be both elating and frustrating? He or she'll have at least some idea if he or she worked with a faculty member on a research project. He or she'll know how frustrating it is when all of the experimental plants die in the greenhouse. Or how elating it can be when he or she comes up with a new interpretation of a poem by Maya Angelou.

An internship that provides hand-on experience in your chosen career is crucial for increasing your competitiveness. A recent study found that up to 75% of organizations hire their interns as full-time workers. Always consider how you can set yourself apart from your peers. You might all be competing for the same job down the line.

Gaining hands-on experience is an important addition to all of the other things you must do to be successful once you leave college. That said, we think that internships and the like are best left until after a student had made the transition from high school to college in his or her first year.

And what if that research or internship experience proves to be a disappointment? It might be that working late nights in the lab with no data to show for your effort fills you with frustration. "Ha," you say, "forget research as a career for me!" That's OK. We think that it is just as valuable for you to know what you *don't* like as it is to know what you *do* like.

WSU has a great resource for connecting students to internships and jobs. It is called Handshake, and you should sign up immediately at www.joinhandshake.com/login. You *must* visit this website! In addition, we recommend going to www.university.linkedin.com, www.linkedin.com/studentjobs, and www.CampusPoint.com.

DANIEL'S STORY

While we just said that internships and the like may be better left until you are more settled as a college student, we think that they are *so* important later that we'll tell you a story. It could be *your* story.

Daniel started at WSU not quite sure of a possible major. At first, Construction Management sounded attractive to him, but without much passion. Daniel took Geology 101 as a lower-division prerequisite course for that major, and simply fell in love with geology. He lived and breathed it. Daniel did research in two geology labs, and was able to request letters of recommendation that attested to his ability and interest. After graduation, Daniel served as a temporary teaching assistant for Geology 101 and then completed a paid internship with a mining company. That internship became a paid contractor position, and that became a full-time job with a very respectable salary. Daniel was competing against about 80 other qualified applicants for that job and now, a few years later, he has achieved his goal of being an exploration geologist. The twist to this story is that the internship and all that followed may not have happened except for a chance conversation in a hallway, which stresses the importance of networking to make contacts. Daniel is a "poster child" for showing where UCORE classes, research, internships, and networking can take you. Oh, and Daniel is also our older son.

ADAM'S STORY

If Daniel's story could be your own story, so could Adam's. Except Adam went to the University of Washington, not WSU.

Adam wanted to study biology, especially ecology, evolution, and conservation. Both during and after his B.S. degree work, Adam gained practical, hands-on experience in organic ag, urban ag, permaculture, and various aspects of plant and animal conservation both in the U.S., and in Central and South America. Today Adam is employed as a restoration ecologist in Laguna Canyon, a little bit north of San Diego. It was Adam's real-world hands-on experience that won him that job out of about 50 other qualified applicants. Adam's story underlines what we also said for Daniel—internships and practical experience can greatly add to your competitiveness. Oh, and Adam is also our younger son.

BEING AN UNDERGRADUATE TEACHING ASSISTANT

At least in the sciences that we know best, Teaching Assistants (TAs) typically are graduate students who run labs and discussion groups under the supervision of a course instructor. And so, a TA has a lot of responsibility, and it isn't a position that should be bestowed lightly.

Some classes will invite exceptional undergraduates to be TAs (they're sometimes called SAs, or Student Assistants). These are students who earned not only superior grades but also demonstrated a high level of interest and motivation, and good communication skills. Serving as an undergraduate TA makes your ability and interest plain for all to see, especially if details are included on your resume and in a letter of recommendation. It also helps consolidate your own understanding of the subject, because you can't be an effective teacher now if you weren't an effective learner before. Jump at the chance of being an undergraduate TA for a class if you earn the opportunity (and some classes offer credit toward graduation, yet one more benefit).

STUDY ABROAD

A semester or two in a foreign country introduces you to new people and new ideas. Among other things, it may enable you to learn or become more proficient in a second language. An understanding of people other than people like you, and an ability (competent if not fluent) to communicate with them, in a culturally-appropriate manner, are skills in high demand in our evermore globally-connected world. Your boss says, "We need someone to install software in our Venice office. Does anyone here speak Italian?" No one raises his or her hand, although you took a few Italian classes at WSU (you could have gone as far as combining studying abroad with a minor in Italian). And you say, "Well, I can speak and write competently, although not really fluently." Guess what? Maybe it's *you* who gets a couple of months in an exciting city in northern Italy, with salary and all expenses paid. Even if the result isn't as dramatic as a few months in Italy, there is some evidence showing that students who study abroad find their first jobs faster and enjoy higher starting salaries than students who stayed home. You can obtain more information on studying abroad by visiting the Office of International Programs at www.ip.wsu.edu.

How about combining studying abroad while doing a service-learning career-related internship? If that combination excites you, check out www.IESabroad.org.

CAREER AND JOB FAIRS

Attending career and job fairs might seem to be only important close to the time when you are graduating, but you should go to them whenever they are offered. First, going as a first-year or sophomore student enables you to see how students closer to graduation go about putting their best feet forward. You'll see what they wear (business or business-casual) and hear how they speak (confident but not arrogant, polished but not overrehearsed). In other words, you'll see and hear how to be a professional job seeker. And second, you might just land yourself an internship, and maybe even one with a salary. As we said earlier, the value of internships, paid or not, can't be overestimated.

NETWORKING

There's an old saying that goes, "It isn't *what* you know it's *who* you know." Both are important in the real world, but the saying does stress the importance of making contacts. Networking is the process by which you connect with people who may be of value to you in terms of gaining internships or your dream job. Networking is something that you might do at a career fair. It is also something that you can do electronically through professional social networking sites such as CareerBuilder, Jobfox, LinkedIn, and VisualCV (to name just a very few—try a search on Google).

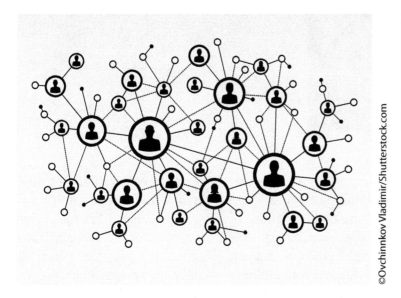

©Ovchinnkov Vladimir/Shutterstock.com

> Networking means making connections with people, the more the better, and can give you a big edge when searching and applying for internships and jobs.

PROFESSIONALISM

At its most basic, being professional means being polite and respectful. You should be these two things to everyone, of course, but be very sure to be as polite and respectful as possible to people whose help you might need, such as instructors and academic advisors. With so much communication done electronically, it is easy to slip into abbreviated text (R U OK?) and the use of sometimes obscure emoji (weirdo facial images). While this is fine for family and friends, you should be more formal with instructors and advisors. We have names that are not "yo" or "hey" or "dude." Use titles like "Ms Smith" or "Dr Jones." Don't use first names unless you've been told that doing so is acceptable. Use an appropriate ending, such as "Best regards, Anne Jones." Words like "please" and "thank you" aren't just nice, they're totally expected.

Along the same lines, be professional when you visit your instructors and advisor during their office hours or scheduled appointments. Be punctual and apologize if you are late, and wait for a bit if you are early. Follow up with an apology if you have a genuine reason for not showing up. Dress appropriately—too-short shorts and torn muscle T-shirts have no place in any office, classroom, studio or lab on campus. Save that attire for the gym or the beach. Please don't chew and crack gum. Don't incessantly check your cell-phone—better yet, just turn it off and put it in your pocket. These things might sound trivial 2 U but they aren't trivial to instructors, advisors, and potential employers. It is largely through respectful actions that you demonstrate your professionalism, the importance of which we cannot stress too much.

©Monkey Business Images/Shutterstock.com

Be professional and polite when meeting with your instructors and your academic advisor. Dress appropriately, and be punctual and prepared.

Remember that what may be acceptable among friends may be very *un*acceptable among professionals. Imagine that you are in contact with an organization that might offer you an internship, or even a job. The CEO calls your cell phone number. Your voice mail greeting of "Hangin' and chillin' so call me back, bro" would be better replaced by "Hello, you've reached Mike. Please leave your number and I'll call you back once I get your message. Thanks." Let's say that you send an e-mail to that organization. Use a professional e-mail address—neither cutiepiegal@yahoo.com nor bigpecsboy@hotmail.com is appropriate unless you want to be a San Diego life-guard. And be careful about what you post on the Web, especially on social media sites. A Facebook photo of you upside down at a keg party with a hose stuck in your mouth is *not* something you want a potential employer to see, trust us. Yes, we probably sound like grumpy old people, but remember: the Web neither forgets nor forgives.

WHAT ARE PREDICTED TO BE SOME OF THE FASTEST GROWING CAREERS IN THE NEXT 10 YEARS OR SO (DATA FROM THE U.S. BUREAU OF LABOR STATISTICS)? NOTE THAT SOME CAREERS REQUIRE TRAINING BEYOND A BACHELOR'S DEGREE

- *Wind turbine technician—108% expected growth: annual median salary approximately $51,000.*
- *Physical therapist—34%: $84,000.*
- *Statistician—34%: $80,000.*
- *Physician assistant—30%: $98,000.*
- *Operations research analyst—30%: $79,000.*
- *Financial adviser—30%: $89,000.*
- *Interpreter/translator—29%: $44,000.*
- *Computer analyst—21%: $86,000.*
- *Software developer—17%: $101,000.*
- *Registered nurse—16%: $67,000.*
- *Physician/surgeon—14%:$187,000.*
- *University professor—13%: $72,000.*
- *Social worker—12%: $46,000.*
- *Accountant—11%: $67,000.*
- *Chef—9%: $42,000.*
- *Lawyer—6%: $116,000 (about average growth).*
- *High-school teacher—6%: $57,000 (about average).*
- *Construction manager—5%: $87,000 (about average).*
- *Aerospace engineer—3%: $108,000 (about average).*
- *Graphic designer—1%: $47,000 (no change).*

WORKSHEET 14
READ: WHY *YOU* BUT NOT *ME*—BEING COMPETITIVE

Let's be honest, the competition to land a job or graduate school position after all of your hard work (and dollars) will be high. So how will your application land you an invitation to interview, how will your interview be memorable, and how will you be a successful intern, graduate student, or employee?

1. Take a moment to reflect on one of your fellow students. List three attributes that he or she has that you think will predict success after graduation in landing a job that has 100 equally-qualified applicants (relevant major and GPA above 3.5). Explain how each attribute will prove valuable.

   a.

   b.

   c.

2. Now think about yourself. What are you good at? What makes you different from any other student in your major? What can you work on so that you are distinctive and your application makes it to the next level? List three attributes, different from the ones above, that you can acquire or improve upon, that just might land you your dream job. For each attribute, explain how you will acquire or improve it. (Remember, there are numerous resources on campus)

   a.

   b.

   c.

Please make and attach a copy of Timetable One from Worksheet One and modify or edit it to reflect your actual timetable during the last week (be honest).

So you've made it! Final exams are almost here or even over, and you're ready for a well-earned break, winter or summer. You've completed at least one semester or close to and your GPA is comfortably above 2.0 (below which you'd be academically deficient, of course). With help from an academic advisor, you are hopefully registered—or getting registered—for your next cohort of classes, if you need more to finish. Graduation is looming just a little bit closer on the horizon. For all of you the question is the same: what are you planning to do over the next vacation: winter or especially (because it is longer) summer? Some of you may have the luxury to just chill or travel. Nice! Others may have found career-related internships, or volunteer or shadowing opportunities. And yet others may need to take a paid job. While we certainly want you to take some time away from academics, if you are able, there are some things that you should be thinking about. To paraphrase what's probably etched into the side-view mirror of your car, the future is closer than you think.

CAREER PLANNING

Some of you may already have a good idea of what you want to do after graduation and the kind of career you'd like to develop. Obviously, the major you choose will be influenced by your goals—and so a B.S. in some kind of engineering would make 100% sense for someone interested in working in a technical position for Boeing in Everett. You may even have mapped out your remaining time at WSU in terms of the classes you intend to take.

But don't put all of your eggs in a single basket. What if that dream job at Boeing fails to materialize? What if you just can't get your GPA to the level that dental schools want to see? The future is uncertain and so you need to develop a Plan B. Ask yourself what kind of careers would fit your interests and goals if you *couldn't* be an aerospace engineer or you *couldn't* be a dentist. Perhaps software design and microbiology might offer good alternatives. Everyone needs to have a Plan B (and maybe even Plans C and D). Even Einstein should have had a Plan B.

But what if you aren't certain of your Plan A let alone your Plan B? When classes are over you'll have more time to do research on what might interest you, and then in the following semester you'll be able to explore your options further with your professors, academic advisor, and folks at the Academic Success and Career Center. Explore some possibilities via www.ascc.wsu.edu/career-services/helpful-links/. Quite a few classes on study methods, major choice, and career planning are offered—look for interdisciplinary classes with a UNIV prefix (e.g., UNIV 101, *College Majors and Career Choice*, and UNIV 301, *College Major and Career Planning*).

Another exercise should be to take one of the many personality and interests tests that are available, if you haven't done so already. Counselors often use the results of such tests to make suggestions about the kinds of careers to which you may be most suited. Perhaps the best known of these tests is the Myers-Briggs Type Indicator, which recognizes 16(!) personality types, and the Strong Interest Inventory. Try Googling both of these—we found a number of websites where you can take these and other tests, although usually for a fee. Alternatively or additionally, you can take a free test, FOCUS2, used by WSU's career counselors. Make an appointment to take this test with the staff in Lighty 180.

As you think about your career interests, be aware of the following expectations that you should have for life after graduation:

- You'll likely be using practices, methods, and even technologies that don't yet exist.
- You may well be working with knowledge that doesn't yet exist.
- You may well be working in a job that doesn't exist yet.
- You'll be learning new skills throughout your career.
- You may well work at several jobs before you retire.

This just emphasizes even further the importance of being flexible and acquiring those all-important transferable skills over your coming few years at WSU.

CHOOSING A MAJOR AND MAYBE A MINOR

Perhaps you knew all along that you wanted to be a history major. Or perhaps it was that history UCORE class you took that triggered your interest in the subject. Regardless, take some time to think about the major in which you'd like to certify, knowing that you can always change your mind (although you wouldn't want to wait too long to do that). Of course, your choice will be influenced by your career goal, as mentioned above. The process named *certification* is an easy one that makes official your chosen area of study and the major in which you will graduate. Students need to have completed at least 24 credits of coursework in order to certify, and some programs may have other requirements, such as additional credits, a minimum GPA, and/or specific classes already taken. WSU offers around 90 different majors, and resources are available to help you make the best choice in terms of your interests and career goals. Among those resources is the Academic Success and Career Center. A really good read can be found at www.exploremymajor/wsu/edu.

What if you choose a major from the 90 or so offered and you change your mind? You'll be in good company—national statistics indicate that about 80% of college students switch their majors at least once, and that switching doesn't much affect graduation rates. Switching is fine, but don't leave it too late. Going from Art to Zoology will be an easier transition if you make it sooner rather than later.

What about minors? A minor is an area outside of your major in which you complete a certain amount of coursework (typically around 20 credits of both required and elective classes). The minor formally acknowledges that you have a level of proficiency in that area, although not as great as for your major (double majors are possible for students with sufficient motivation: talk with your advisor). WSU offers nearly 100 minors, and we encourage you to explore whether a minor might be right for you. It might satisfy your curiosity now or it might add to your competitiveness in the future. We think that minoring in a foreign language is a great idea for students who are interested in going beyond a few years of, say, Spanish or French in high school. We live in a truly global world, and being able to communicate in a foreign language, competently if not fluently, might mean that it's *you* who gets to work at the corporate office in Madrid or Paris (if you're able, studying abroad can only further increase those odds). Along these same lines, combining a major in molecular biology with a minor in business administration might be a good move for someone interested in developing a biotechnology company.

©Vichie81/Shutterstock.com

> *What if taking a minor in Spanish could result in a paid trip to, or even job in, Madrid?*

PLANNING FUTURE CLASSES

This is easiest when you are pretty certain of your major, of course. What classes would or might you take looking out toward graduation? Many students and advisors like to develop a four-year plan early in a student's college career. We certainly think it is valuable to look at least a few semesters into the future. But remember that courses on offer today might not be offered down the line and that new ones might become available. And your interests may change a little. Anticipate the need for some future flexibility in any plans you develop now.

While it would be extremely unwise to compromise your performance in WSU classes, we do suggest that you take a look at supplements that exist on-line. For example, Lynda.com (from LinkedIn) offers more than 2,000 video tutorials that help you to develop a diverse portfolio of creative, business, and technology skills. And an ever-increasing number of jobs require some competence in writing software code. Just Google "jobs that use computer coding," and then Google places where that kind of training is available, sometimes at no or little cost. Instead, or as well as, check out our own computer science classes-CPT_S 111 (*Introduction to Computer Programming*) would be a good start.

SEARCHING FOR INTERNSHIPS AND SCHOLARLY OPPORTUNITIES

As we discussed earlier, engaging in internships and scholarly activity can add greatly to your competitiveness after graduation. While we don't believe that most first-year students should be involved in such activities as they transition to college life, we do think that it is never too early to start thinking about them. Do some research to be as sure as possible that any internship you undertake will have the highest value—don't regard completing an internship as just one more hoop to jump through on the road to graduation. Find out what kinds of experiences would be most beneficial. For example, perhaps a would-be applicant to vet school would benefit from volunteering in a vet clinic (a 100% benefit, we'd say). Hunt around and see what opportunities might be available (and they don't have to be in Pullman), and make necessary contacts as early as you can. Oh, and internships can earn you academic credit toward your degree requirement. We provide some additional information on available resources in Chapter 14.

All of the same holds true for research. For an overview of undergraduate research at WSU, a great first-stop is www.undergraduateresearch.wsu.edu. From there, check out faculty pages on the WSU website and make contact with people whose research sounds interesting. Tell them a bit about you—your experience, skills, and goals—and ask if you can meet face-to-face. But be sure to do some "pre-research research" before that meeting so that you'll be totally prepared. And research can earn you academic credit toward your degree requirements.

©Hxdbzxy/Shutterstock.com

The production of new understanding, knowledge, and ideas might be lab work in the sciences, and creative activity in the arts and humanities.

Many people consider research to be something done only by scientists, but that isn't true if we think more generally about what academics call "scholarly and creative activity." This involves the generation of new understanding, knowledge, and ideas across all disciplines, certainly not just science. Are you a music major interested in the place of the trumpet in jazz? Then explore the different playing styles of Louis Armstrong and Miles Davis, and you'll be engaging in *scholarly* activity (their styles differ quite a lot). Or maybe you play the trumpet yourself. Then compose something new by writing your own blues or ballad, and you'll be engaging in *creative* activity.

FINDING GRANTS AND SCHOLARSHIPS

While loans are useful, of course (perhaps even crucial for some people), there are other sources of funds to which you can apply to help pay your way through college. Grants and scholarships are especially nice because, unlike loans, they don't need to be repaid. Now, that doesn't mean you can spend your scholarship money on whatever you like, such as a trip to Florida for Spring Break or a new Corvette. You'll be constrained in what you can buy—textbooks perhaps, or tuition. But who doesn't like free money? And for the most competitive scholarships, being awarded one is a great resume builder that will only increase your odds of achieving your career goal.

Take some time to search for scholarships for which you might be eligible (try Google—you'll be amazed at just how diverse the breadth of eligible applicants can be at the national level). WSU scholarships range from institution-wide to college- or department-specific, and you can find more information on scholarships in general (WSU's and others) at www.financialaid.wsu.edu/scholarships.

FINDING A MENTOR

You have received and will receive in the future lots of help from many different people at WSU. They include instructors, TAs, tutors, academic advisors, the folks in financial aid—the list is long. These people are there to help you solve specific, short-term problems. "What classes should I take as a pre-law student?" "Help me understand Camus' philosophy of the absurd." "When will I receive my financial aid check?"

But a mentor is different. Rather than coaching and training you in specific areas, a mentor helps you in the longer-term as you grow and move toward your goals, both personal and professional. Mentors also act as role models, and may be faculty, staff or even your more-experienced peers. Talk to an academic adviser about how you might find a mentor.

SOME FINAL WORDS

It seems never ending, doesn't it? We believe that your four years as a student at WSU should be more than just eight semesters out of your (very long?) life. We believe that you should be thinking, planning, and working across all 48 months to put yourself in the best position for what you aim to achieve after college. Life doesn't end when you graduate. Many of you are now making the transition from high school to college. For others, you're closer to making the transition from college to career. You may be just a semester or two away from graduation. To all of you we say work hard and smart—and a little good luck never hurts!

WORKSHEET 15
READ: LOOKING TO THE FUTURE

1. List three different majors that interest you and give a reason for each of your choices. For each choice, what kind of careers are you thinking about?

   a.

   b.

   c.

2. You may not have considered doing a minor. Check out minor requirements on the WSU website and list three different ones that might interest you, giving a reason for your interest.

   a.

   b.

   c.

3. Do you know that the Associated Students of Washington State University (ASWSU) provides free newspapers in the CUB? (well, it does in the spring of 2017) Get a freebie newspaper (or access one online or buy one if you have to), find an article in it that interests you, and write a summary below (no plagiarism!). Will you use this newspaper as a resource in the future, perhaps in a class you take? Why yes or no?

4. Now look at all of the weekly timetables you have produced. Was the timetable exercise valuable? Did managing your time get easier? List four things that you learned while making and revising your timetable.

   a.

   b.

   c.

   d.

INDEX